There is a hard law…
When an injury is done to us,
we never recover until we forgive.

ALAN PATON

Why Forgive?

JOHANN CHRISTOPH ARNOLD

THE PLOUGH PUBLISHING HOUSE

Published by The Plough Publishing House
Walden, New York
Robertsbridge, England
Elsmore, Australia
www.plough.com

Why Forgive? is a revised and expanded version of Arnold's book *Seventy Times Seven* (1997), which simultaneously appeared in Great Britain as *The Lost Art of Forgiving.*

Softcover: ISBN 978-0-87486-852-4

FIRST UK PRINTING, APRIL 2008: 5,000
SECOND UK PRINTING, MAY 2008: 5,000
THIRD UK PRINTING, OCTOBER 2008: 5,000
FOURTH UK PRINTING, DECEMBER 2008: 2,000
FIFTH UK PRINTING, APRIL 2009: 5,000
SIXTH UK PRINTING, NOVEMBER 2011: 5,000
SEVENTH UK PRINTING, AUGUST 2012: 7,000
EIGHTH UK PRINTING, JUNE 2013: 7,000
NINTH UK PRINTING, OCTOBER 2013: 10,000

To protect the privacy of individuals who contributed to this book, several names have been changed. Where a name appears without a surname, it is a pseudonym. Other names are real.

A catalogue record for this book is available from the British Library.

Library of Congress Cataloging-in-Publication Data

Arnold, Johann Christoph, 1940 -
    Why forgive? / Johann Christoph Arnold.
      p. cm.
Rev. ed. of: Seventy Times Seven. Includes index
    ISBN: 0-87486-992-7 (alk. paper)
    1. Forgiveness--Religious aspects--Bruderhof Communities. I. Arnold, Johann
Christoph, 1940- Seventy times seven. II. Title.
    BV4647.F55 A76 2000
    234'.5--dc21

                                                                99-050827
                                                                CIP

Printed and bound by CPI Group (UK) Ltd, Croydon, CR0 4YY

CONTENTS

FOREWORD

It was the summer of 1999, in Northern Ireland, that I first met Steven McDonald, a New York City police officer. As fellow participants in a sort of peace pilgrimage organised by *Breaking the Cycle*, we travelled from one powerful event to the next, hearing stories from people on both sides of the Troubles, who were sick and tired of bloodshed. Everywhere we went, Detective McDonald was asked to tell his story too: how he had wound up in a wheelchair, paralysed from the neck down, and why he was so sure that forgiveness and reconciliation were the keys – the only keys – to a new era of peace.

I won't relate Steven's story here – you can find it for yourself toward the end of this book. But I will say this: what impressed me most was Steven's insistence that there are "more stories of love and forgiveness in the world than there are of hatred and revenge," and that deep down, each of us has one to offer.

This book is a collection of such stories. It's not a how-to book, or a religious guide. The book's sole purpose is to let ordinary people speak for themselves – people whose experiences have given them the right to talk about over-coming hurt and pain.

"Hurt" is an understatement, actually, because many of their stories deal with much bigger things: brutal crimes, financial betrayal, sexual abuse, and racial bigotry. Others deal with the sort of everyday challenges that every one of us can relate to: negative gossip, tensions at work, strained friendships, and the way the happiest marriage can grow cold.

As in life, not all of the stories have happy endings. A few show what happens to people who refuse to forgive, or simply cannot, no matter how hard they try. Others address the difficulty of forgiving oneself, and the fruitlessness of blaming God.

I can relate to the latter in a very personal way. In November 1980, my wife was expecting our fourth child. Just two weeks before the due date, she sensed that something was wrong: in fact, she could no longer feel the slightest movement. The next two days went by at an agonising crawl as we spent hours at a local hospital waiting for test results. Throughout, we felt as if being jerked between hope and despair.

Then, on the evening of 29 November, my wife gave birth to a stillborn baby boy. We named him Johann. He was perfect, but our hearts were empty of any joy. After all those months of waiting, what had gone wrong? Was it somehow our fault? All in all, Johann's arrival brought on a flood of self-accusations and a wave of resentment toward God. How could he have allowed this?

Eventually we could no longer deal with our bitterness – it was eating us up – and turned to a family counsellor for help. After we had told him what we were going through, he told us he believed that nothing happens without a purpose, and that even if that purpose wasn't clear to us, we ought to let its mystery draw us closer to one another, rather than tear us apart…

Back to Steven McDonald, let me conclude these thoughts with something he once said about why it's so important to forgive. He was speaking to an auditorium full of teens, and he told them that it was probably the hardest thing they'd ever attempt to do. He then added:

> But once you are able to let go of wrongs that have been done to you, it changes everything. It will change your relationships, your attitudes, your emotional make-up – your whole approach to living. It will give you a better life. Plus, you'll find that when you forgive, you're always a winner. You don't lose a thing. I know this will sound illogical or impossible to some. Others will find it down-

right ridiculous. But I'm talking as one who has lived through this: Forgiving is the most beautiful expression of love. It's not a sign of weakness. It's a sign of strength.

By the time you finish this book, perhaps you will be able to say the same. Why forgive? Read these stories, and decide for yourself.

John W. Fransham
Robertsbridge, East Sussex

PROLOGUE

One morning in September 1995, as I sat drinking coffee and reading the paper, I was horrified to see headlines reporting the abduction, in broad daylight, of a local seven-year-old girl. Within a week the primary suspect – a trusted acquaintance of the child's family – confessed to the crime. After luring her into a wooded area near her home, he had raped her, beaten her to death, and hidden her.

The public's reaction was predictable: this man deserved to die. Under the state's new capital punishment statute, he was regarded as a prime candidate. Initially the District Attorney promised to seek a maximum of twenty years in exchange for information leading to the recovery of the girl's body, but he went back on his word after it was found, saying he would have made a pact with the devil to find the child. He also said that he hoped to become the first DA in recent New York history to send a murderer to the death chamber. Residents interviewed by the local news media even suggested that the authorities release him so they could "take care of him."

While this rage was understandable, I wondered how it could possibly bring solace to the victim's grieving family.

As a pastor, I felt fairly certain what my response should be: I arranged for someone from my congregation to go to the funeral, and I sent flowers to the child's parents. I tried (unsuccessfully) to visit the family. But my heart was still heavy. Somehow, I felt I had to visit the murderer – at this point still a faceless monster – and confront him with the horror of his actions. I wanted to help him see that if he was ever going to find peace with himself after committing such a heinous crime, it could only be through lifelong remorse.

I knew people would look askance at such a visit, if not entirely misinterpret it, but I was convinced it was my duty. So it was that a few months later I found myself sitting alone in the county jail, face to face with the uncuffed killer. The hours I spent in that cell shook me deeply and left many unresolved questions – questions, in fact, that eventually led me to write this book.

Less than three months after my visit, the murderer faced his victim's family in court. The room was packed, and entering it, one could feel a wave of hostility. First the sentence – life imprisonment without parole – was read out, and then the judge added: "I hope that the hell you now face in prison is only a foretaste of the hell you will face in eternity."

The defendant was then allowed a few words. In a loud, wavering voice, he told the girl's parents that he was "truly sorry" for the pain he had caused – and that he was praying daily for forgiveness. As a ripple of angry whispers spread through the audience, I asked myself, How can such a man ever be forgiven?

The Cancer of Bitterness

Resentment is like drinking poison and then
hoping it will kill your enemies.

NELSON MANDELA

Forgiveness is a door to peace and happiness. It is a small, narrow door, and cannot be entered without stooping. It is also hard to find. But no matter how long the search, it *can* be found. At least that is what the men and women in this book have discovered. By reading their stories, perhaps you, too, will be led to the door of forgiveness. Just remember that once there, only you can open it.

What does forgiving really mean? Clearly it has little to do with human fairness, which demands an eye for an eye, or with excusing, which means brushing something aside. Life is never fair, and it is full of things that can never be excused.

When we forgive someone for a mistake or a deliberate hurt, we still recognise it as such, but instead of lashing out or biting back, we attempt to see beyond it, so as to restore our relationship with the person responsible for it. Our forgiveness may not take away our pain – it may not even be acknowledged or accepted – yet the act of offering it will keep us from being sucked into the downward spiral of resentment. It will also guard us against the temptation of taking out our anger or hurt on someone else.

It is only natural, when we are hurt, to want to revisit the source of that hurt. There is nothing wrong with that. Whenever we do this in the sense of chalking up another person's guilt, however, our pain will soon turn into resentment. It doesn't matter if the cause of our pain is real or imagined: the effect is the same. Once there, it will slowly eat away at us until it spills out and corrodes everything around us.

We all know bitter people. They have an amazing memory for the tiniest detail, and they wallow in self-pity and resentment. They catalogue every offence and are always ready to show others how much they have been hurt. On the outside they may appear to be calm and composed, but inside they are about to burst with pent-up feelings.

Bitter people defend their grudges constantly: they feel that they have been hurt too deeply and too often, and that this exempts them from the need to forgive. But it is just these people who need to forgive most of all. Their hearts are sometimes so full of rancour that they no longer have the capacity to love.

Over thirty years ago my father and I were asked by a colleague to visit an acquaintance who claimed she could no longer love. Jane's husband lay dying, and she longed to comfort him, yet something seemed to hold her back from within. Jane was by all accounts a blameless person: she was neat, meticulous, capable, hard-working, and honest – yet in talking with her it became clear that she was as unfeeling as a rock. She really could not love.

After months of counselling, the cause of Jane's coldness finally became clear: she was unable to forgive. She couldn't point to a single large hurt, but emotionally she was tied down – in fact, almost completely incapacitated – by the collective weight of a thousand small grudges.

Thankfully Jane was later able to overcome herself and rediscover the joy of living. That was not the case with Brenda, another embittered woman I attempted to counsel. Sexually abused by her uncle for years and silenced by her alcoholism, which her tormentor supported with daily gifts of vodka, she had finally escaped from him, but she was still under his thrall.

When I met Brenda she had been offered intensive psychiatric counselling. She also had a good job and an extensive network of supportive friends, who had made every effort to get her back on her feet. In spite of this she seemed to make no progress. Her emotions swung widely, from excited laughter to inconsolable weeping. She binged on food one day and fasted and purged the next. And she drank – bottle after bottle.

Brenda was without question the innocent victim of a horribly depraved man, yet the better I got to know her the more it seemed that she was perpetuating her own misery. In refusing to lay aside her hatred for her uncle, she was continuing to let him exert his influence over her.

Brenda was one of the most difficult people I have ever tried to help. Again and again I tried to get her to see that until she could forgive her uncle – or at least see beyond the fact that he had abused her – she would in effect remain his victim. But my efforts were in vain. Increasingly angry and confused, she drove herself deeper and deeper into a jungle of despair. Finally she attempted to strangle herself and had to be hospitalised.

The wounds left by sexual abuse take years to heal. Often they leave permanent scars. Yet they need not result in life-long torment or in suicide. For every case like Brenda's there are others where, through forgiving, the victim is able to find happiness and a new lease on life.

By the time Glenn Fielder was sixteen, the East London teen was both a record-holding track champion, and an aspiring football player with Leyton Orient FC – the same club where David Beckham started out before signing for Manchester United. But while Beckham went on to enjoy international fame, Fielder, who grew up on the same street and has close ties with the superstar to this day, woke up one day to find out that he had been paralysed for life.

It was January 1987, and I'd been invited to a party at a community hall in Chingford. I'd been looking forward to it, and had a great time. Shortly before midnight I left with a friend and walked into a fracas involving seven or eight guys. We turned aside and kept walking – we didn't want to get involved, but a hundred yards or so down the road we came across a young man lying in the gutter, so we stopped. He'd been badly beaten. I bent down to put my coat under his head, and my friend ran into a nearby building to call an ambulance.

While we were waiting for help to come, the fight grew louder and louder behind us. As it grew nearer, I got a little nervous, and stood up. As I did, I felt this short, sharp punch in my back, and fell unconscious. It was actually a knife, plunged right between my shoulder blades. I'm told that after I was stabbed, I was savagely beaten and stomped by three or four guys. But I don't remember any of that. I only know that when I woke up, I was lying in a hospital with a severed spinal cord. I'd been there two or

Glenn Fielder

three weeks, under sedation, when I started coming to, and that's when my father broke the news to me that I was going to spend the rest of my life in a wheelchair.

My world ended at that point – I felt as though my heart had been ripped from inside of me. Football was my life, and now I'd never be able to play again. I couldn't imagine anything worse. When I came out of the hospital eleven months later, I was still in a state. Even thinking about

6

football was devastating. I ripped up old team photos and threw away medals. I couldn't bear to watch games on TV.

Six young men were arrested in connection with Glenn's assault. One of them, an 18-year-old, was given a six-year sentence, though he only did four years behind bars. Not surprisingly, Glenn was enraged. "Six years for an unprovoked attack? Where was the justice in that? I'd just been sentenced for life – to lifetime disability. I wanted revenge, and that desire embittered me and filled me."

After almost a year, Glenn was finally able to move home and embark on the long journey of trying to put back together some semblance of a normal life:

It was a good hospital – Stokes Mandeville – with one of the best rehab units in England. They did their best to prepare me for life as a paraplegic. But to be honest, I felt my life was finished. In the end, my better nature prevailed. I went after various jobs. At first I worked in the civil service, which I didn't enjoy. I was an outdoor person. But what choice did I have? I then moved on to a stationery company, where I did sales. During that time I met my wife, Julie, and settled down.

Through it all, I had to deal with what was going on inside me. You see, people who'd see me knew right away that I was disabled, and if they asked, I'd tell them it was due to a knife attack. But what I could never tell them about – what they could never see – was the anger that burned inside of me. I stewed for years. I'd lie in bed plotting my attacker's death, fantasising about what I was going to do.

Meanwhile, people were always saying things like, "It's so unjust. If I were you, I'd have had that bloke's legs blown off, blah, blah, blah." These people thought they were helping me by saying this, but in fact, all they were doing was making things worse, fuelling my anger and stressing me even more.

Luckily, something held me back from taking revenge. I don't know what it was, but thank God it held me back. And eventually I found myself getting to where I could tell myself, "Hold on a minute. At least you're still alive. You're married to a beautiful woman; you've got two beautiful children. You have your own job (I drive a hand-controlled taxi for a living), and your own house, and you manage to pay all your bills."

I guess I saw that I was actually leading a better life than my attacker was. You see, I had been told quite a bit about him: he'd been in and out of prison all his life and was a drug user with psychiatric problems. His family was ashamed of him. And look at me! I found myself thinking, "If you can't get rid of your anger from the inside out, you're never going to be able to really move on." So I decided to try to forgive. Now, don't get me wrong. It's not something that happened overnight. I'm a very proud man. I could never have walked up to this guy in the street and say, "I forgive you." But I *began* to forgive him, over a period of time. And gradually – it wasn't an instant reaction – I felt better. You could say I was slowly healed.

Not long ago my younger brother Danny called me and said, "Glenn, I've got news for you. That guy that attacked you? He's been found dead. I reckon what goes around comes around, eh?" I said, "You know what, Danny? I feel nothing. I feel empty. I'm actually sorry for his family. There's no bitterness anymore – I've moved on with my life."

As Glenn's life (and countless others) shows, forgiving always involves the conscious decision to stop hating, because hating can never help. Contrary to the simplistic proverb "forgive and forget," however, it does not necessarily require forgetting. Who can cast off the memories of a childhood marked by abuse; and how can someone in a wheelchair possibly forget that he or she will never walk again? Nor does it need to involve confronting the perpetrator. In the case of sexual trauma, this is probably not even advisable. Still, for some people, a face-to-face reckoning may prove to be the only way forward. And it may yield a life-changing surprise, as illustrated by the next story.

"Life is ten percent what happens to you, and ninety percent what you do with it." The speaker was my friend Charles Williams, a retired police chief (and teacher of criminal justice studies) from a small town, and he was addressing a panel of educators from the local school district.

As I listened, I remembered the first time I met him. It was at a high school assembly on the topic of nonviolent conflict resolution, and Chief Williams, as he is known, had been dumbfounded by the story of the featured speaker – a victim of violent crime who had forgiven his assailant. In his own words:

> I thought, "Wow what a great message – teaching kids how to deal with conflict in a nonviolent manner. I was mesmerised." On the other hand, I was saying to myself, "There's no way, no freaking way I ever could forgive something like that. It's not possible; I'd be too angry about it, too mad." Later I was telling someone about the assembly, and I said, "Explain this forgiveness thing to me. I just don't understand it." We talked, and it suddenly hit me that the reason I couldn't see someone else forgiving a violent crime was that I myself had someone I needed to forgive, but couldn't. That person was my mother.
>
> You see, I grew up in an alcoholic household. My mother was a raging alcoholic, and when I say raging, I mean pots and pans being thrown. I can remember her throwing chairs, and saying, "Stop the world! I want to get off!" One time she wrenched herself out of her coat as my father tried to stop her running off. He didn't manage, and she was gone for two days. We didn't know whether she was dead or alive.
>
> By the time I was an adult I was angry. I was angry at her for years. And I'll be the first to tell you that I enjoyed being angry at her. And even after I finally realised

that I needed to forgive my mother, it took me five years. But I finally did. It was a Tuesday, and I drove down to Long Island, back to my hometown, and called my mother when I was about fifteen minutes away. I got her answering machine. I thought, "Perfect – now I have an excuse not to do this." I almost turned around. But something deep inside told me,

Charles Williams

"No – now is the time." So I left her a message. Before I knew it, she called back.

To make a long story short, I went into the house and sat down, and forgave the woman who made my childhood a nightmare. I can tell you one thing: it wasn't easy. On the other hand, this person in front of me – this person who was, in my mind's eye, a crazed monster with a wild look in her eyes – instantaneously changed into a frail, sickly, old woman on oxygen, dying of emphysema. She became the mother I had never had.

Again, it wasn't easy to forgive her. Because when I say I hated her, I *hated* her. It affected me as an individual; it affected my marriage to the point that my wife and I separated. It affected my ability to be a good father. It tainted everything.

Shortly after this, Chief Williams's mother was diagnosed with a brain tumour, and metastatic lung cancer. She was ready for a fight, as her son tells it, and part of it was her determination to have a second chance at her relationship with her son.

She said, "I want to make it right." I told her, "Mom, I forgive you. You don't have to make anything right." Anyway, she went through radiation, and then one day I got a call from my sister. She said, "You better come. Mom's not doing well." So I flew down and walked into the hospice where she was staying. When I walked into the room I could hardly recognize her. It wasn't her, really. She had lost her teeth, and had barely any hair left. Worse, she was blind, and could hardly speak or move.

I walked over and said, "I forgive you, Mom, and I love you," and she smiled. Then I added in my best Long Island accent, "Ma, I love what you done wit' your hair." Next thing I know, she's cursing me out from head to toe! Now, no words came out of her mouth, but she did this – believe me – so I knew she was really still there.

Then I sat down next to her and I told her again how much I loved her. Who knew – it might be the last time I'd see her, and as much as I had hated her in the past, I now loved her just as much. If that's hard to understand, it's because there is sometimes a fine line between love and hate.

I was crying by then, like a baby – like a son who's about to lose his mother. Meanwhile, Mom, who hadn't moved the whole time I was there, suddenly lifted her arm and stroked my hand three times. Twenty-four hours before her death, and *she* is consoling *me*.

That's what I choose to remember about my mother. But understand this: had I not forgiven her beforehand and worked to repair the damage that had been done, I never would have had that moment.

Bitterness, as the previous story shows, is more than a negative outlook on life. It is a power – and a destructive and self-destructive one at that. Like a cancerous cell, a dangerous mould, or a spore, it thrives in the dark recesses of the heart and feeds on every new thought of spite or hatred that comes our way. And like an ulcer aggravated by worry or a heart condition made worse by stress, it can be physically as well as emotionally debilitating. In fact, if not addressed and taken care of, bitterness can lead to death. Hence the ancient Chinese proverb attributed to Confucius, "Who opts for revenge should dig two graves." Tragically, that is what Anne Coleman, a Delaware woman I have known for years, experienced firsthand:

> One day in 1985 I picked up the phone to hear my niece in Los Angeles say, "Anne, Frances has been shot. She's dead."
>
> I can't remember screaming, but I did. I made plans to fly out to California immediately, and on the plane I really thought I could kill someone. If I'd had a weapon and the murderer, I probably would have done just that.

Daniel, Anne, and Frances Coleman

By the time I got off the plane I was getting concerned about how I was going to greet my son Daniel, who was flying in from Hawaii. Daniel was an army sergeant, and he had been trained to kill.

When we got to the police station the next morning, the only thing they told us was that my daughter was dead, and that everything else was none of our business. Sadly, this remained the case throughout the days we stayed in Los Angeles. The violent crimes coordinator told me that if they hadn't arrested someone in four days, I shouldn't expect an arrest: "We just have too many homicides in this precinct – we spend only four days on homicides."

This enraged my son Daniel. When he found out that the police department was really not interested in finding his sister's killer, he said he was going to go out and buy an Uzi and mow people down.

They hadn't really prepared us for what we would see when we picked up her car from the pound. Frances had bled to death in her car. The bullets had passed through her aorta, her heart, both lungs. She had choked on her own blood. She died early on a Sunday morning, and we picked up the car late Tuesday afternoon. It stank. That smell never left Daniel's mind, and he wanted vengeance in the worst way. He really wanted someone to do something – some kind of justice for his sister.

Over the next two-and-a-half years I saw Daniel go downhill, and then I stood alongside his sister's grave to watch him being lowered into the ground. He had finally taken revenge – on himself. I saw what hatred does: it takes the ultimate toll on one's mind and body.

Believe in Miracles

Hope for a great sea-change
on the far side of revenge.
Believe that a further shore
is reachable from here.
Believe in miracles
and cures and healing wells.

SEAMUS HEANEY

Gordon Wilson held his daughter's hand as they lay trapped beneath a mountain of rubble. It was 1987, and he and Marie had been attending a peaceful memorial service in Enniskillen, Northern Ireland, when a terrorist bomb went off. By the end of the day Marie and nine other civilians were dead, and sixty-three had been hospitalised for injuries.

Amazingly, Gordon refused to retaliate, saying that angry words could neither restore his daughter nor bring peace to Belfast. Only hours after the bombing, he told BBC reporters:

> I have lost my daughter, and we shall miss her. But I bear no ill will. I bear no grudge...That will not bring her back... Don't ask me, please, for a purpose...I don't have an answer. But I know there has to be a plan. If I didn't think that, I would commit suicide. It's part of a greater plan... and we shall meet again.

Later Gordon said that his words were not intended as a theological response to his daughter's murder. He had simply blurted them out from the depth of his heart. In the days and weeks that followed the bombing, he struggled to live up to his words. It wasn't easy, but they were something to hang on to, something to keep him afloat in the dark hours when grief overwhelmed him.

He knew that the people who took his daughter's life were anything but remorseful, and he maintained that they should be punished and imprisoned. Even so, he refused to seek revenge.

> Those who have to account for this deed will have to face a judgement of God, which is way beyond my forgiveness... It would be wrong for me to give any impression that gunmen and bombers should be allowed to walk the streets freely. But...whether or not they are judged here on earth by a court of law...I do my very best in human terms to show forgiveness...The last word rests with God.

Gordon Wilson

Gordon was misunder-stood and ridiculed by many because of his stand, but he says that without having made a decision to forgive, he never could have accepted the fact that his daughter was never coming back. Nor could he have found the freedom to move on. Forgiving also had a positive effect that reached beyond his personal life. At least temporarily, his words broke the cycle of killing and revenge: the local Protestant paramilitary leadership felt so convicted by his courage that they did not retaliate.

If Gordon's ability to forgive as quickly as he did seems admirable, it is also unusual. For most of us – as for Piri Thomas, a writer known for his memoir, *Down These Mean Streets* – forgiveness does not come so easily:

> Whenever I hear the phrase "forgive and forget," my thoughts flow back to the forties and fifties, to the ghet-tos of New York. There, where violence was and still is a part of life, so many times I heard people who had been

wronged refuse when they were asked for forgiveness. Or, they would compromise with "OK, OK, I'll forgive you, but I sure won't forget."

I have been among the countless who have made that same angry promise. I remember the painful trauma I suffered when my mother Dolores passed away. She was thirty-four, I was seventeen. I got very angry at God for not letting my mother live, and refused to forgive God for being so inconsiderate. As time went by, I forgave God, but for a very long time I couldn't forget because of the great pain alive in my heart.

At the age of twenty-two, I became involved in a series of armed robberies with three other men. In the commission of the last armed robbery, there was a shoot-out with the police. I was shot by one of the officers, whom I shot in return. The policeman recovered. Otherwise I would not be writing this article, for I would have been put to death in the electric chair at Sing Sing.

While I was recovering in the prison ward of Bellevue Hospital, one of the three gunmen, a man named Angelo, turned state's evidence against me. Angelo was like a brother to me. We had both grown up on the same block of 104th Street. Angelo ratted on me about some past unarmed robberies because detectives at the 23rd Precinct threatened to beat him up so badly that even his own mother would not be able to recognize him. Angelo held up for as long as he could and then spilled out to the detectives what was and never was. When I was released from Bellevue Hospital, I was incarcerated in the Manhattan Tombs to await trial, where I found out that all that Angelo had confessed to had been dumped on me...

To make a long story short, I was sentenced to five to ten and five to fifteen years to run concurrently, at hard labor, first at Sing Sing and then at Comstock.

From time to time over the years, I would steam with anger over Angelo's betrayal, which had led to two armed robbery warrants hanging over me in the South Bronx. In my cell at night I would find myself fantasising on ways to kill him or at least hurt him so bad he would beg for death. Angelo and I had been tight brothers from the streets. I loved him as such, but now in prison I hated him and only wanted to get even with him in the worst way. To tell the truth, I fought against these murderous feelings over the years and even prayed to get those violent thoughts out of my mind. Sometimes for long periods of time, I would forget all about Angelo, but when least expected, thought of his betrayal would pop up inside of me.

I was finally released in 1957 and was ordered to report to both a parole officer and a probation officer each week. Back out in the streets, I couldn't help thinking what would happen if I ran into Angelo. I never went looking for him because I really didn't want to find him.

I was attending a small church on 118th Street, utilising it as a half-way house to keep me free from the gravity of those mean streets. I would think about Angelo from time to time and feel the anger still alive in my heart. I never met up with him and found better things to occupy my mind, like working on the book I started in prison, meeting a young woman named Nelin, and feeling the joy of falling in love with Nelin and sharing the same warm feelings. Angelo began to diminish and slowly fade away from my mind.

One balmy summer evening we were walking on Third Avenue. Nelin and I were happily checking out jewellery stores, pricing engagement and wedding rings. As we left one jewellery store for another, I heard someone softly call out my name: "Oye, Piri." I knew without a doubt that the voice belonged to Angelo. I turned to look. His once young face now showed deep lines of stress, caused perhaps by having to look so often over his shoulder. I felt the rumbling of some long-ago anger trying to rise like bile out of my guts. I suppressed the urge and waited patiently to listen to whatever Angelo had to say.

Nelin pulled at my arm to get my attention and then asked me with her eyes if this was the man I had mentioned with so much anger. She whispered, *"Por favor,* Piri, don't forget what we have talked about."

I nodded and turned back to Angelo, who swallowed hard, not so much out of fear but rather as if he badly needed to get something out that he had been waiting to say for a very long time. His voice was soft.

"Piri, I have hurt everybody I loved, and that sure includes you. In the police station they began to beat me so bad, I couldn't take it. Could you please forgive me for ratting, bro?"

I stared at him, wondering how he could have the nerve to be calling me bro after ratting on me, but at the same time happy to be called bro by him once again.

"I will understand if you don't, but it took this long for me to build up my nerve. And even if you don't, I still had to try, so *por favor,* what do you say, Piri?"

I stared at Angelo and only answered when I felt Nelin squeeze my hand. The words that came from my heart lifted a great weight from my soul, and I felt my spirit soar free.

"Sure bro, I forgive you. They say everybody's got a breaking point, and that includes me. So on God's truth, Angelo, I not only forgive you, bro, it's also forgotten and to that I swear on Mom's grave."

The tears that exploded from Angelo's eyes matched my own.

"*Gracias,* Piri. For years I've hated my guts for not having the heart to keep from ratting on you. If I could live that all over again, I would let them beat me to death rather than turn on you. *Gracias,* bro, for your forgiving and forgetting, and I mean that from my heart."

Angelo put his hand out and then started to draw it back, as if not wanting to push his luck. My right hand reached out quickly and shook his hand with great sincerity and I felt Angelo squeeze my own. We hugged briefly, and then with a smile he nodded to me and Nelin, and said "See you around, bro" and then walked away. I put my arm around Nelin's shoulders, she slipped her arm around my waist, and we both watched Angelo as he disappeared

Piri Thomas

around the corner. I couldn't help thinking about something Nelin once told me she had read: "To err is human, to forgive divine."

It sure is hard to forgive, but as my father Juan often said, "Everything is hard until you learn it, and then it becomes easy." I had learned. I had not only forgiven my street brother Angelo, but I had also learned to forgive myself for having carried a thirst for revenge for so many years. I felt like the morning sunrise was coming up in my heart. I took Nelin's hand in my own and with smiles we headed towards the next jewellery store. Love in me was at last free from the weight of hate.

I never saw my bro Angelo again, for he moved to another city, and it was with sorrow that I learned some years later that he had been murdered because of money he owed a loan shark.

But I will always be glad that I forgave Angelo. I have learned that the cruellest prison of all is the prison of an unforgiving mind and spirit.

Sometimes, even when we recognize the need to forgive, we are tempted to claim that we cannot. It is simply too hard, too difficult – something for saints, maybe, but not the rest of us. We have been hurt just one time too many, we think, or misunderstood. Our side of the story has not been adequately heard.

To me, the amazing thing about Gordon and Piri's stories is that they did not weigh their options, but decided to forgive on the spur of a moment, and did so from the bottom of their hearts. If they hadn't, they might never have been able to forgive at all. Of course, not everyone is able to forgive with such decisiveness or speed. But as the next story shows, that does not detract from the power of the act.

Hashim Garrett once roamed the streets of Brooklyn with a gang – and a loaded gun. Today he is a well-known motivational speaker at schools across the country, and the owner of his own consulting firm, Wisdom and Understanding. As a result of a shooting when he was fifteen, he is almost completely paralysed from the waist down, and walks only with great effort, and a pair of crutches. Strangely, he says he's come to see that incident not as a bad day, but as "one of the best days of my life, because it helped me to see things clearly, and gave me a new lease on life." To some, such an attitude may seem nearly impossible to understand. To Hashim however, it has a simple explanation – one that has everything to do with forgiveness.

Growing up in Brooklyn, I spent a lot of time hanging out. My friends were mostly older kids who didn't think learning was cool, and before long I was making bad decisions. I wouldn't have called them "bad" at the time, because at that stage I was fascinated by all the things these older guys were about. They didn't go to school. They had a lot of girls. It seemed they always called their own shots. I liked that. My mother always told me that I shouldn't hang around these guys, but I was fifteen. I didn't need her guidance anymore; I knew it all. I'd say, "I hear you, Ma." But I still didn't care.

Next thing you know, my "friends" and I are getting into arguments. You see, when I first started hanging out with them, I'd do whatever they told me to do. If they said to go beat somebody up, I'd go do it. I wanted to show them how much heart I had. I was doing a lot of other bad stuff too. Then, as time went on, they'd tell me to do even worse things, and I'd say, "I'm not gonna do it." So we started bumping heads. Some "friends" will love you only as long as you do what they want you to do.

They always told me we should carry guns, "just in case." The idea was that if you ran into trouble, you'd have protection. One day – it was May 7, 1990 – we were out walking to the corner store, and I had this odd feeling, and then all of a sudden the guy walking next to me shouted, "Look out! Run!" I ran, and I kept running, but then I turned, and I saw this kid with a submachine gun (it turned out to be a Tech 9). Then my jeans made a funny movement, and something hit me hard, in my back. I didn't realise it at the time, but the movement my jeans made was a bullet going through my leg, and the pain in my back was another bullet.

I fell down to the ground, and when I tried to move, I couldn't. I couldn't even feel my legs. I was totally alone. My friends had all run for their lives. I closed my eyes. I was scared out of my mind. I was sure the kid with the gun was going to come up close and kill me. Then I opened my eyes, and he was gone.

Aside from the two bullets Hashim felt, there were four more. All in all, six bullets passed through him, leaving a total of twelve entry and exit wounds.

While I lay on the ground, bleeding to death and looking up at the sky, I called out, "God, *please* don't let me die." I could feel in my heart that he would hear my prayer; I was full of conviction. As the words left my tongue, it was as if the world had blinked. By "blinked" I mean that up to that moment, I was so frightened that my heart was pounding. As soon as I uttered those words, though, I couldn't even remember my fear. Everything changed. I was suddenly calm. As a believer, I now know why: when you call out to the Creator, peace and tranquillity come over you.

Then all of a sudden, somebody was putting a jacket under my head, and two of my friends were there, arguing about whether to try and move me. I told them to try moving me, and they began pulling me up. As soon as they did, something popped, so they let me back down again...

Hashim Garrett

What Hashim felt was presumably something in his lower spine. In any event, he was left paralysed from the waist down. He spent much of the next year in a New York City hospital, thinking about how to get even with his assailant, and twisting his hair (he has not cut his hair since the day of his shooting, and keeps it in dreads as a reminder of that time):

Revenge consumed me. All I could think about was, "Just wait till I get better; just wait till I see this kid." When the investigators came to my bedside and told me they knew who had shot me, I said, "That's not him; let him go," because I wanted to exact revenge myself. They said, "What do you mean? We know it's him." They didn't want me going and taking things into my own hands. I tried to reassure them. I lied, "Don't worry, I'm not going to do anything."

As days turned into weeks, I got angrier and angrier. I cried. I couldn't sleep. I didn't feel like eating. I refused my medication. All I wanted was to get well enough to go kill this kid for shooting me. I didn't even know him, but I was consumed by wanting to know what he had shot

27

me for. (Eventually I found out: he'd shot me because my friends had set me up. You see, we weren't getting along anymore. They'd loved me as long as I was willing to do stupid things with them.)

Then, as time went on, I began to think differently. I said to myself, "If I take revenge on him, I can only imagine what God is going to put me through." I'd started feeling that God was trying to teach me a very important lesson, and that I'd better take it seriously. I also reasoned that if I harmed this young man, something bad would come back to me. You see, six months before this happened, *I* had shot a kid, for no reason except that a friend told me to do it and I wanted to prove how tough I was. Six months later, I am shot by somebody because *his* friend told *him* to do it. Whatever you put out in this world – whatever you do – will always come back to you. It must. It's just a matter of time.

My journey through all this is still hard for me to describe. How do you tell someone what it feels like to be totally helpless? What it's like to need help going to the bathroom when you're *fifteen*? That you're never going to be able to walk on your own again, no matter how many times you tell everyone you're sorry for the bad decisions you made? It's almost impossible to convey the pain I was in at the time, and I'm not just talking about the physical pain. That was off the charts. But the confusion, the mental agony, the inner pain – nothing could have prepared me for it. I *ached* inside. It was hell on earth, and there was no appealing it; no way around it. I was going to be stuck with the consequences of my choices forever.

In the end, though, I decided to forgive. I felt God had saved my life for a reason, and that I had better fulfill that purpose. I didn't know what it was, but I sensed God had something special in mind for me. And I knew that I could never go back out there and harm someone. I was done with that mindset, and the lifestyle that goes with it: an eye for an eye, and the continual little (and big) beefs.

I came to see that I had to let go and stop hating. I began to realise that the time we have with each other on this earth is borrowed time, and made up my mind that when my soul leaves this shell, my good deeds are going to outweigh my evil ones. I also learned that if you have forgiveness in your heart, bad things may still happen, but a bad thing can be a blessing in disguise.

I didn't just have to work on forgiving the kid who shot me. There were also my "friends" – those kids who had set me up, who felt my life was expendable. I had to forgive them as well. And then I had to forgive myself, and the Creator, because at one point I felt, "God, I was terrible – why didn't you just let me die instead of putting me through all this."

It was like I had an epiphany: something came to me as I was lying there in the hospital and told me I should forgive. If I hadn't, I'm not sure I'd be here today. I definitely wouldn't be traveling the globe, speaking to teens about making the world a better place.

Hashim's story reminds us that forgiveness can break the cycle of violence in the most unlikely places, like the destitute inner-city neighbourhood where he grew up. So does the next one. In opening a window on two lives touched by the deadliest conflict of our time – the war in Iraq – it offers hope that even a battleground can yield seeds of peace and lead us, as the verse that opens this chapter puts it, to "the far side of revenge."

In spring 1998, Carroll and Doris King – old family friends – travelled to Iraq with a human rights delegation to examine the effects of the UN sanctions there. While in Baghdad they met Ghaidaa, a woman who had suffered more than any mother I had ever heard of, but was still ready to forgive.

Ghaidaa lost nine children in the destruction of Al Amariyah, a massive, reinforced concrete shelter in Baghdad that was penetrated by American "smart bombs" during the Gulf War. More than one thousand Iraqi civilians were incinerated in the bombing, most of them women and children.

Today, Ghaidaa leads tourists among the shelter ruins, hoping that those who see its horrors – among other things, ghostly silhouettes were left wherever human bodies shielded the walls from the extreme heat – will speak out against future bombings. After taking one of Ghaidaa's tours, Carroll and Doris, stunned, asked her to forgive them for what America had done to her family and people. A former Air Force officer who had flown bombing sorties over Europe in World War II, Carroll especially felt he bore a share of the guilt. Shaking his hand, then hugging Doris and bursting into tears, Ghaidaa cried, "I forgive you."

Ghaidaa will never find "justice" on human terms. How can one ever replace nine dead children? She will certainly never be able to forget them. But in finding the hearts of two people who asked her to forgive them, she has found peace – something that no one can put a price on.

Ending the Cycle
of Hatred

If only there were evil people somewhere insidiously committing evil deeds, and it were necessary only to separate them from the rest of us and destroy them! But the line dividing good and evil cuts through the heart of every human being. And who is willing to destroy a piece of his own heart?

ALEKSANDR SOLZHENITSYN

Recited by millions from childhood on, the Lord's Prayer includes the plea, "Forgive us our debts, as we forgive our debtors." Familiar as it is, I often wonder whether we really mean what we say when we repeat these words, and whether we sufficiently consider their meaning. To me, at least, they imply that once we recognise our own need for forgiveness, we will be able to forgive. This recognition does not come to most of us easily, because it demands humility. But isn't humility the essence of forgiveness?

In a chapter of the Gospel of Matthew known as the Beatitudes, we are told that the meek will be blessed and inherit the earth. And in the parable of the unmerciful servant, he warns us not to treat others any more harshly than we would want to be treated:

A rich man wanted to settle accounts with his servants. One of them, who owed him several thousand pounds, was brought in front of him, unable to pay. Because he was defaulting on the loan, the rich man ordered that the servant should be sold into slavery, together with his wife and children, to repay the debt. Although the rich man was within his legal rights to demand this, the servant begged him for patience. So the rich man took pity on him. He cancelled the debt and let him go. But the experience left the servant badly shaken, worried about the state of his finances, and no sooner had he returned home than he went to a friend, who still owed him a small amount of money, and demanded repayment. His friend was also unable to pay, and begged the servant for mercy, but he refused. Instead, he had his friend thrown into prison.

When the other servants saw what he had done, they were very upset and told the rich man everything. The rich man was furious, and called him in to answer for his actions: "You begged me to cancel your debt, so I did. Why didn't you show the same level of mercy to your friend as I showed to you?" In his anger, the rich man turned him over to the jailers to be tortured, until he could pay back all he owed.

In my experience, the strongest motivation for forgiveness is always the sense of having received forgiveness ourselves, or – if we do not have that – an awareness that, like everyone else in the human race, we are imperfect and have done things we need to be forgiven for.

Jared, an African-American student from Boston, says that was definitely the case with him:

> I was six years old when I awoke to the reality of racism: from the sheltered environment of my home, I was pushed out into the world – a local primary school just down the road from our house. I went there for only a month before city law mandated that I be bussed across town to another school. My parents were not happy with this; they wanted me to go to a school where I was known and loved. They owned a farm out in the country, and so we moved there...
>
> My father, a veteran of the civil rights movement, taught me love and respect for everyone – white or black. They tried to teach me not to see everything in life along racial lines. All the same, I was the only black child in my new school, and many of the other children had obviously been taught to hate.
>
> Children can be brutal about each other's differences. They may begin with an innocent question – "Why is your skin brown?" – but then they start to laugh at you and mock you, because somewhere along the line they have been taught that if you're different – not "normal" – there's something wrong with you.

I was a fish out of water, and these kids didn't make it easy for me. I'll never forget one especially painful incident: I introduced one of my white friends to another white kid on the bus one day, and from then on they always sat together but left me out.

Later I moved to a different school, and by the time I was twelve, the tables had turned completely. Our class was now all black, except for one white guy in my class, Shawn, who was the only white in the whole school. We treated him as an outcast and taunted him with racial epithets and physically abused him. We took out our hatred of white people on him even though he hadn't done anything to harm any of us. We were angry.

Shawn symbolised everything that we knew about whites and their history: the humiliation of our people, the lynchings, the mobs, and the slave trade. We took out all our bitterness and anger on him.

I was never able to apologize to Shawn. By the time I saw my racism for what it was, we had parted ways. But I did ask God to forgive me for the harm I caused Shawn, and I resolved to forgive the guys who didn't have a heart for me when I was the only black kid in their midst.

Hela Ehrlich, a Jewish friend, has a similar story. Hela grew up in Nazi Germany, and though her immediate family escaped the death camps by emigrating just before the

Hela Ehrlich

outbreak of World War II, her grandparents on both sides and all her childhood friends lost their lives in the Holocaust.

For many people, the passage of time softens heartache; for Hela, the opposite occurred. Slowly, almost imperceptibly, her hurt turned into bitterness, and her pain into anger. Hela did not want to be bitter; she wanted to be free to live and love. In fact, she struggled constantly to keep from hardening her heart. But she could not forgive.

Then one day it dawned on her: she would never be able to forgive her family's executioners until she was able to see that despite their guilt, they were still fellow human beings.

> Trembling, I realised that if I looked into my own heart I could find seeds of hatred there, too. Arrogant thoughts, feelings of irritation toward others, coldness, anger, envy, and indifference – these are the roots of what happened in Nazi Germany. And they are there in *every* human being.
>
> As I recognised – more clearly than ever before – that I myself stood in desperate need of forgiveness, I was able to forgive, and finally I felt completely free.

Josef Ben-Eliezer, another friend, had a similar journey. Born in Frankfurt, Germany, in 1929, he is the son of Polish Jews who fled their homeland to escape persecution and poverty, but found little respite from either:

> My first memory of anti-Semitism is from when I was three years old. I was standing at the window of our house on the Ostendstrasse when a formation of Hitler Youth marched past, singing *Wenn Judenblut vom Messer spritzt* ("When Jewish blood runs from our knives"). I still remember the horror on my parents' faces.
>
> Our family soon decided to leave the country, and by the end of 1933 we had moved back to Rozwadow, Poland. Most of its inhabitants were Jews: artisans, tailors, carpenters, and merchants. There was a great deal of poverty, but under the circumstances we were considered middle-class. We lived in Rozwadow for the next six years.
>
> In 1939 the war started, and within weeks the Germans entered our town. My father and older brother hid in the attic, and whenever someone knocked at our door and asked for them, we said they were not at home.
>
> Then came the dreaded public announcement: all Jews had to gather in the town square. We were given only a few hours. We took whatever we could carry in bundles on our backs. From the square, the SS forced us to march toward a river several miles from the village. Uniformed men rode alongside us on motorcycles. One of them stopped and shouted at us to hurry up, then came up to my father and struck him.

At the riverbank other uniformed men were waiting for us. They searched us for money, jewellery, and watches – they did not find the sum of money my parents had hidden in my little sister's clothing – and then ordered us to cross the river, into a no-man's-land. They did not instruct us what to do after that, so we found lodging in a nearby village.

A few days later we suddenly heard that the far side of the river was also going to be occupied by the Germans. We panicked, and with the money we had hidden, my parents – together with two or three other families – bought a horse and wagon to carry the younger children and what little we had managed to bring along on our backs.

We travelled east toward Russia, hoping to reach the border before dark, but found ourselves in a large forest when night fell. During the night we were attacked by armed thugs who demanded we hand over everything we had. It was a frightening moment, but luckily the men in our caravan had the courage to resist them, and in the end our attackers left, taking only a bicycle and a few other small items.

Josef spent the next years in Siberia, from where he escaped to Palestine in 1943. After the war he met Jews who had survived the concentration camps:

When the first children freed from Bergen-Belsen and Buchenwald began to arrive in Palestine in 1945, I was horrified to hear what they had gone through. They were young boys – twelve, thirteen, and fourteen years old – but

Josef Ben-Eliezer

they looked like old men. I was devastated, and filled with hatred for the Nazis...

Then the British began to restrict the immigration of Holocaust survivors to Palestine, and I was filled with hatred for them too. Like other Jews, I promised myself that I would never again go like a sheep to slaughter, at least not without putting up a good fight. We felt we were living in a world of wild beasts, and we couldn't see how we would survive unless we became like them.

When the British mandate in Palestine came to an end, we no longer had them to fight, but we did have the Arabs, who wanted "our" land. That was when I joined the army. I could no longer allow myself to be trampled on...

During one campaign, my unit forced a group of Palestinians to leave their village within hours. We didn't allow them to leave in peace, but turned on them out of sheer hatred. While interrogating them, we beat them brutally and even murdered some of them. We had not been ordered to do this but acted on our own initiative. Our lowest instincts had been released.

Suddenly, my childhood in wartime Poland flashed before my eyes. In my mind I relived my own experience as a ten-year-old, driven from my home. Here, too, were people – men, women, and children – fleeing with whatever they could carry. And there was fear in their eyes, a fear that I myself knew all too well. I was terribly distressed, but I was under orders, and I continued to search them for valuables...

Josef was no longer a victim, but his new position on the side of power brought him no peace. In fact, it did the opposite. Again and again, the memory of his own suffering ate at him and brought new waves of guilt.

Josef left the army, but he still wasn't happy. He abandoned Judaism, and then religion as a whole. He tried to make sense of the world by rationalising its evils. But even that didn't seem to work. It was only through his discovery of the "real" Jesus, he says – "someone who has very little to do with all the violence that is carried out in his name" – that he realised the freedom of a life lived without hatred.

In my heart I heard Jesus' words, "How often did I want to gather you, and you would not." I felt the power of these words and knew that it could unite people across every barrier – people of all nations, races, and religions. It was an overwhelming experience. It turned my life upside down, because I realised that it meant the healing of hatred, and the forgiveness of sins.

In my new faith, I have experienced the reality of forgiveness. And I ask myself, "How, then, can you not forgive others?"

Like Josef, and like so many others on both sides of the Arab-Israeli conflict, Bishara Awad, a Palestinian acquaintance of mine, has been wounded by his share of injustices. Speaking about his life-long struggle to forgive, he once told me:

> In 1948, during the terrible war between the Arabs and the Jewish settlers, thousands of Palestinians died and many more became homeless. Our own family was not spared. My father was shot dead by a stray bullet, and there was no decent burial place. No one could leave the area for fear of getting shot at by either side; there was not a priest nor a minister to say a prayer. So Mother read to us from the Bible, and the men who were present buried my father in the courtyard. There was no way they could have taken him to the regular cemetery in the city.
>
> Mother thus became a widow at the age of twenty-nine, and she was left with seven children. I was only nine years old. For weeks we were caught up in the crossfire and were unable to leave our basement room. Then one night, the Jordanian army forced us to run to the Old City. That was the last time we ever saw our home and our furniture. We ran away with nothing but the clothes on our backs, some of us only in pyjamas...
>
> In the Old City we were refugees. We were put in a kerosene storage room that had no furniture. A Muslim family gave us some blankets and some food. Life was very hard; I still remember nights when we went to sleep without any food.

Mother had been trained as a nurse, and she got a job at a hospital for $25 a month. She worked at night and continued her studies during the day, and we children were put in orphanages.

My sisters were accepted in a Muslim school, and we boys were placed in a home run by a British woman. To me, this was a real blow. First I had lost my father, and now I was away from my mother and my family. We were allowed to visit home once a month, but otherwise we stayed at the boys' home for the next twelve years. Here, with my two brothers and eighty other boys, my suffering continued. We never had enough to eat. The food was terrible and the treatment harsh.

As an adult, Bishara went to school in the United States and became an American citizen. Later he returned to Israel and took a job teaching in a Christian school. Looking back, he says:

That first year I was very frustrated. I did not accomplish much and I felt defeated...There was mounting hatred against the Jewish oppressors: all of my students were Palestinians, and all had suffered in the same way I had...I wasn't able to help my students, because of the overriding hatred in me. I had harboured it since childhood without even realising it.

One night I prayed to God in tears. I asked forgiveness for hating the Jews and for allowing hatred to control my life...Instantly he took away my frustration, hopelessness, and hatred and replaced it with love.

Bishara Awad

In a culture that emphasizes self-preservation and individualism, forgiveness is scoffed at so routinely that most people never stop to really consider its potential to heal wounds such as the ones Bishara described, or to lift the burden of their memory. Instead they sit tight: cramped, trapped, unable to move forward. Whether they do so out of a conscious refusal to forgive, or are simply unable to let go of their pain, it doesn't matter. Either way, they remain inwardly bound. And in the end, there is only one answer to their torment: to keep the hope of freedom in front of them, and to go on believing for them when they lose heart. To quote Naim Ateek, a Palestinian priest in Jerusalem whose life story mirrors Bishara's in several ways:

> When people hate, its power engulfs them and they are totally consumed by it...Keep struggling against hatred and resentment. At times you will have the upper hand, at times you will feel beaten down. Although it is extremely difficult, never let hatred completely overtake you...

Never stop trying to live the commandment of love and forgiveness. Do not dilute the strength of Jesus' message; do not shun it; do not dismiss it as unreal and impractical. Do not cut it to your size, trying to make it more applicable to real life in the world. Do not change it so that it will suit you. Keep it as it is, aspire to it, desire it, and work for its achievement.

Indeed, far from leaving us weak and vulnerable, forgiveness is empowering, both to the person who grants it and the one who receives it. In bringing relief to the most difficult situations, it allows us to lay aside the riddles of retribution and human fairness, and to experience peace of heart. Finally, it sets into motion a positive chain reaction that passes on the fruits of our forgiveness to others.

Bless Your Persecutors

At some thoughts one stands perplexed – especially at the sight of men's sin – and wonders whether one should use force or humble love. Always decide to use humble love. If you resolve to do that, once and for all, you can subdue the whole world. Loving humility is marvellously strong, the strongest of all things, and there is nothing else like it.

FYODOR DOSTOEVSKY

In a passage of the Gospels known as the Sermon on the Mount, Jesus teaches us not only to love our enemies, but even to "bless" those who persecute us. It wasn't just a sermon. As his unmistakably compassionate plea from the cross shows – "Father, forgive them, for they know not what they do" – he practiced what he preached. So did Stephen, the first Christian martyr, who prayed much the same thing as he was being stoned to death: "Father, do not hold this against them."

Many people dismiss such an attitude as self-destructive foolishness. How and why should we embrace someone intent on harming or killing us? Why not fight back in self-defence? When I showed an earlier version of this book to a prison inmate I've corresponded with for years, he reacted in just this way:

> I cannot imagine myself ever asking the oppressed – whether Jews, Native Americans, or any other persecuted peoples throughout history – to forgive their oppressors. Who can dare?
>
> I hear you answer: "Jesus!" But when I look at the Jews, I see that it was precisely the followers of Jesus – so-called "Christians" – who became their deadliest enemies, who herded them into the ghettos of Europe, and when the ghettos filled, into the ovens of Auschwitz, while millions of Christians stood by in silence. As for the Native Americans, this nation pushed them to the edge of extinction, herded them into reservations, onto the worst lands.
>
> It's easy for folks who live in a virtual paradise, who have enough to eat, farms, land, nice homes, businesses, etc., to preach about forgiveness. But is it really fair to say that to people who live in hellholes – jobless, threatened by imminent death by starvation – people who are, as Frantz Fanon put it, "the wretched of the earth"? Are they to forgive the fat, well-fed millions who voted for their starvation? Who voted for war? Who voted for prisons? Who voted for their perpetual repression? Who wish, in their heart-of-hearts, that these wretched ones

were never born? Should they forgive them for the repression to come? For the genocide that is to come?

"Lord, forgive them for what they do, even though they and their ancestors have been doing it for five hundred years..." Can you really embrace such a prayer?

It is for this reason that my heart has been called to political action: to change hellish realities, and to try to transform this world from the hell it is for billions of her inhabitants. Change those conditions, and then perhaps forgiveness can be born.

These words may seem overly harsh to some, but they are significant because their writer holds a perspective unlike that of anyone else in this book. Some twenty-five years ago, in a politically charged trial whose fairness is still being debated in higher courts, he was convicted of murder – many say framed – and sentenced to death. If there is anyone who has a lot to forgive, it is this man. His challenge – how dare the "Christian" world expect forgiveness from the oppressed, while turning a blind eye to the systems of injustice that hold them down – is a valid, vital one. To me, it is answered, at least in part, by a saying attributed to Francis of Assisi: "Preach the gospel at all times. If necessary, use words." In relation to forgiving, this thought brings home an essential issue: so long as we merely theorize about it, admire it, or demand it of others, forgiveness is meaningless. Its real power (as the next story shows) is unleashed only when we are willing to actually practice it.

After more than thirty years working with lepers in India, Gladys Staines, a nurse, and her husband Graham, a missionary, had seen plenty of death and dying. But nothing could have prepared her for the night in January 1999 when her husband and their two sons, Philip (10) and Timothy (6) failed to return home from a religious retreat – or for the day after, when news came that their bodies had been found in the family jeep, burned beyond recognition. Nor were the friends who stood with her that harrowing morning prepared for her response. According to a report in *The New York Times:*

> Mrs. Staines shook with grief and, for a time, moved very slowly, as if struggling to part her way through the air. She seemed to be impaled in the middle of a thought, which finally, with quavering voice, she shared. "Whoever did this, we will forgive them," she said.
>
> That sentiment – that example of her living faith – has been widely praised in India, a nation often rent with religion-based violence, most frequently between Hindu and Muslim. D. P. Wadhwa, a Supreme Court judge heading an inquiry into the deaths, and their link to a wider outbreak of anti-Christian attacks, commended Mrs. Staines. "By her conduct, she has put to shame, if they have any shame, not only the perpetrators of the crime but all those who directly or indirectly may have sympathy for them," he said.
>
> Mrs. Staines...has decided to carry on her husband's work, running a home for leprosy patients here in Baripada,

Gladys and Graham Staines with Philip, Timothy and Esther

a dusty, traffic-clogged city in the eastern state of Orissa. And she will continue to tell people the "good news," as she confidently calls it, that...God is fair and just, and that divine purposes exist in all that goes on, even if those purposes are at times elusive.

Indeed, she has yet to fathom why God has taken her sons and husband. Questions leap into her mind – a tumble of thoughts – but she tries to set them aside rather than pursue answers. "I ask myself, do I dwell on the type of death they had? Were they killed first or burned alive? Am I angry? Am I not? I don't know. I cope by not allowing myself to do much thinking. At times I am overcome with sadness. They're not here. I can't play with my boys. Day by day, I start with the Bible, reading prayers. Previously, I could talk to my husband before going to bed. Now I talk to God, pour out my heart to Him, and He gives me the strength and wisdom to go on."

Of those who murdered her husband and boys, she went on, "I can forgive their deeds, but I cannot forgive their sins. Only Jesus can forgive their sins. And they will have to ask."

After the funeral, which was attended by thousands, Mrs. Staines and her 13-year-old daughter, Esther, the family's two survivors, faced the throng that had accompanied them to the cemetery and sang a favourite hymn. "Because He lives, I can face tomorrow," the words went. "Because He lives, all fear is gone."

Though unfathomable to many, Gladys Staines's understanding of forgiveness is not unheard of. It has been embraced by countless persecuted minorities throughout history, from the earliest Christian believers, to the Anabaptists of the radical Reformation, to our century's followers of Tolstoy, Gandhi, and Martin Luther King. It is probably best explained in this passage from King's book *Strength to Love:*

Probably no admonition of Jesus has been more difficult to follow than the command to love our enemies. Some people have sincerely felt that its actual practice is not possible. It is easy, they say, to love those who love you, but how can one love those who openly and insidiously seek to defeat you...?

Far from being the pious injunction of a Utopian dreamer, the command to love one's enemy is an absolute necessity for our survival. Love even for our enemies is the key to the solution of the problems of our world. Jesus is not an impractical idealist; he is the practical realist...

Returning hate for hate multiplies hate, adding deeper darkness to a night already devoid of stars. Darkness cannot drive out darkness; only light can do that. Hate cannot drive out hate; only love can do that. Hate multiplies hate, violence multiplies violence, and toughness multiplies toughness in a descending spiral of destruction...

Love is the only force capable of transforming an enemy into a friend. We never get rid of an enemy by meeting hate with hate; we get rid of an enemy by getting rid of enmity. By its very nature, hate destroys and tears down; by its very nature, love creates and builds up. Love transforms with redemptive power.

King's commitment to love as a political weapon grew out of his faith, but there was a good streak of pragmatism in his thinking as well. He knew that he and other African-Americans involved in the civil rights movement would have to live for decades to come with the same people they were now confronting. If they let their treatment embitter them, it would soon lead to violence, which would only lead to new cycles of repression and embitterment. Rather than breaking down the walls of racial hatred, it would build them higher. Only by forgiving their oppressors, King said, could African-Americans end the "descending spiral of destruction." Only forgiveness could bring about lasting change:

We must develop and maintain the capacity to forgive. Whoever is devoid of the power to forgive is devoid of the power to love. It is impossible even to begin the act of loving one's enemies without the prior acceptance of the necessity, over and over again, of forgiving those who inflict evil and injury upon us.

It is also necessary to realise that the forgiving act must always be initiated by the person who has been wronged, the victim of some great hurt, the recipient of some tortuous injustice, the absorber of some terrible act of oppression. The wrongdoer may request forgiveness. They may come to themselves, and like the prodigal son, move up some dusty road, their heart palpitating with the desire for forgiveness. But only the injured neighbour, the loving father back home, can really pour out the warm waters of forgiveness.

Forgiveness does not mean ignoring what has been done or putting a false label on an evil act. It means, rather, that the evil act no longer remains as a barrier to the relationship. Forgiveness is a catalyst creating the atmosphere necessary for a fresh start and a new beginning...

To our most bitter opponents we say: We shall match your capacity to inflict suffering by our capacity to endure suffering. We shall meet your physical force with soul force. Do to us what you will, and we shall continue to love you.

We cannot in all good conscience obey your unjust laws, because noncooperation with evil is as much a moral obligation as is cooperation with good. Throw us in jail, and we shall still love you. Send your hooded perpetrators of violence into our community at the midnight hour and beat us and leave us half dead, and we shall still love you. But be ye assured that we will wear you down by our capacity to suffer.

One day we shall win our freedom, but not only for ourselves. We shall so appeal to your heart and conscience that we shall win you in the process, and our victory will be a double victory.

Martin Luther King

In the spring of 1965 I marched with King in Marion, Alabama, and experienced firsthand his deep love and humility in the face of injustice. I was visiting the Tuskegee Institute with colleagues from New York when we heard about the death of Jimmie Lee Jackson, a young man who had been shot eight days earlier when a rally at a church in Marion was broken up by police. State troopers from all over central Alabama had converged on the town and beaten the protesters with clubs as they poured out onto the streets.

Bystanders later described a scene of utter chaos: white onlookers smashed cameras and shot out street lights, while police officers brutally attacked black men and women, some of whom were kneeling and praying on the steps of their church.

Jimmie's crime was he'd tackled a state trooper who was mercilessly beating his mother. His punishment: to be shot in the stomach and clubbed over the head until almost

53

dead. Denied admission at the local hospital, he was taken to Selma, where he was able to tell his story to reporters. He died several days later.

At the news of Jimmie's death, we drove to Selma immediately. The viewing, at Brown Chapel, was open-casket, and although the mortician had done his best to cover his injuries, the wounds on Jimmie's head could not be hidden: three murderous blows, each an inch wide and three inches long, ran above his ear, at the base of his skull, and on the top of his head.

Deeply shaken, we attended a memorial service there. The room was packed with about three thousand people (many more stood outside), and we sat on a window sill at the back. We never heard one note of anger or revenge in the service. Instead, a spirit of courage emanated from the men and women of the congregation, especially as they rose to sing the old slave song, "Ain't gonna let nobody turn me 'round."

Later, at a second service in Marion, the atmosphere was decidedly more subdued. Lining the veranda of the county court house across the street stood a long row of state troopers, hands on their night sticks, looking straight at us. These were the same men who had attacked Marion's blacks only days before. The crowd of whites gathered at nearby City Hall was no less intimidating. Armed with binoculars and cameras, they scanned and photographed us so thoroughly that we felt every one of us had been marked.

Afterwards, at the cemetery, King spoke about forgiveness and love. He pleaded with his people to pray for the police, to forgive the murderer, and to forgive those who were persecuting them. Then we held hands and sang, "We shall overcome." It was an unforgettable moment. If there was ever cause for hatred or vengeance, it was here. But none was to be felt, not even from Jimmie's parents.

Not long ago I read about a remarkable act of forgiveness by the children of Selma in those same days of early 1965. Local students had organized a peaceful after-school march when the town's notorious Sheriff Clark arrived. Clark's deputies began to push and prod the children, and soon they were running. Initially the boys and girls thought the sheriff was marching them toward the county jail, but it soon became clear that they were headed for a prison camp almost five miles out of town. The men did not relent until the children were retching and vomiting. Later they claimed they wanted to wear out Selma's "marching fever" for good.

A few days after this incident, Sheriff Clark was hospitalised with chest pains. Unbelievably, Selma's school children organised a second march outside the court house, chanting prayers for his recovery and carrying get-well signs.

Eminent child psychiatrist Robert Coles observed the same remarkable attitude of forgiveness among children when he was working in New Orleans in 1960. White parents, openly opposed to a federal court decision that ended segregation in the city's schools, not only withdrew their children from any school that admitted blacks, but picketed these schools as well.

One child, six-year-old Ruby Bridges, was the sole African-American student at her school, which meant that for a while she was also the only student there. For weeks she had to be escorted to school by federal marshals. One day, her teacher saw her mouthing words as she passed the lines of angry white parents hurling abuse. When the teacher reported this to Coles, he was curious: What had she said?

When asked, Ruby said that she had been praying for the parents of her white classmates. Coles was perplexed. "But why?" "Because they need praying for," she answered. She had heard in church about Jesus' dying words, "Father, forgive them, for they know not what they do," and had taken them to heart.

Through James Christensen, the prior of a Trappist monastery in Rome, I recently learned of a remarkable story of someone who not only forgave his persecutors, but did so before the fact. In May 1996, the GIA, a radical Muslim faction active in Algeria, kidnapped seven of James's fellow Trappists in the Atlas Mountains and threatened to hold

them hostage until France released several of their own imprisoned compatriots. Several weeks passed, and still the
French government refused. In the end, the GIA killed the
monks by beheading them.

All France was horrified, and every Catholic church in
the country tolled its bells at the same time in the monks'
memory. What struck me most about the tragedy, however,
was something that had quietly foreshadowed it two years
before. The prior of the Algerian monastery, Christian de
Chergé, had had a strange premonition that he would soon
die a violent death, and wrote a letter forgiving his future
assassins, sealed it, and left it with his mother in France.
Opened only after his murder, it read in part:

> If it should happen one day – and it could be today – that
> I become a victim of the terrorism that now seems to en-
> compass all the foreigners living in Algeria, I would like
> my community, my church, my family, to remember that
> my life was given to God and to Algeria; and that they
> accept that the sole Master of all life was not a stranger to
> this brutal departure.
>
> I would like, when the time comes, to have a space of
> clearness that would allow me to beg forgiveness of God
> and of my fellow human beings, and at the same time to for-
> give with all my heart the one who will strike me down.
>
> I could not desire such a death; it seems to me impor-
> tant to state this: How could I rejoice if the Algerian peo-
> ple I love were indiscriminately accused of my murder?

My death, obviously, will appear to confirm those who hastily judged me naïve or idealistic: "Let him tell us now what he thinks of it!" But they should know that...for this life lost, I give thanks to God. In this "thank you," which is said for everything in my life from now on, I certainly include you, my last-minute friend who will not have known what you are doing...I commend you to the God in whose face I see yours. And may we find each other, happy "good thieves" in Paradise, if it please God, the Father of us both.

Who was de Chergé, and what was the source of his deep convictions regarding peace and forgiveness?

According to a book about his religious order, *The Monks of Tibhirine,* it all began in 1959, when de Chergé was sent to Algeria with the French Army's "pacification" forces. While there he befriended Mohammed, a Muslim policeman, and together they took weekly walks to discuss politics, culture, and theology. One subject that came up again and again was the tense relationship between Algeria's Christians (its French colonisers) and Muslims (its native population). On one of these walks, a squad of Algerian rebels ambushed the two men. De Chergé, wearing his army fatigues, was sure his end had come. Then Mohammed stepped in between his friend and the attackers and told them to leave de Chergé alone: "He is a godly man." Amazingly, they let both men go. But this act of bravery cost Mohammed his life: he was found murdered in the street the next day.

The episode gripped de Chergé for days – and completely changed his life. He decided to commit himself to God and to the cause of peace. When his tour of duty ended he returned to France and entered a Trappist monastery. Later he studied to become a priest and asked to be transferred to an Algerian base. This wish was granted and he moved back to Africa, eventually becoming the ecclesiastical head of a rural district in the Atlas Mountains.

Christian de Chergé

As abbot, de Chergé made decisions that his overseas superiors saw as unusual and even unwise. Instead of simply evangelising, he offered the locals employment, medical care, and lessons in literacy and French. He also organised an annual interfaith summit to promote Muslim-Christian dialogue. He even invited Muslims to stay at the compound of Notre-Dame de l'Atlas, his monastery. By this, de Chergé aimed to show the world that Muslims and Christians can live together under one God or Allah. As he explained it, "the only way for us to give witness is...to be what we are *in the midst of banal, everyday realities.*"

Over time, despite de Chergé's efforts – or perhaps because of them? – the GIA grew angry with the Trappists, whom they saw as meddlers. So it was that they were finally kidnapped, held hostage, and murdered.

To many people, the death of de Chergé and his fellow monks proves the worst stereotypes of Islam. But to him it was the expected cost of being a peacemaker. To me, it is a stark reminder of the work that must be done worldwide to spread the healing message of forgiveness. In a time when so many people are willing to die in ongoing armed conflicts between the "Christian" West and the supposed "menace" of Islam – whether in Iraq, Afghanistan, Algeria, or anywhere else – where are there men and women who are willing to die for the sake of peace? Certainly de Chergé was one of these. To quote once more from his remarkable farewell letter:

> I know the caricatures which a certain Islamic ideology encourages and which make it easy for some to dismiss the religion as hateful...But such people should know that at last I will be able to see the children of Islam as He sees them – He whose secret joy is to bring forth our common humanity amid our differences.

Forgiveness and Justice

Truth without love kills, but love without truth lies.

EBERHARD ARNOLD

David, an Israeli acquaintance, experienced hardships similar to those of Hela and Josef, in Chapter 3, but offers a somewhat different viewpoint. David's story raises an age-old question posed by generations of suffering men and women over the course of human history: Are there no limits to forgiveness?

I was born in Kassel, Germany, in 1929, the fateful year of the financial and economic crash that had such a decisive impact on world affairs and was instrumental in bringing the Nazis to power in Germany...My father was a journalist; mother an educator. Our family was well off, and life was happy until the clouds of fascism began to accumulate.

Like many Jews throughout the country, father did not take the Nazis too seriously at first. How could the solid, cultured Germans fall for that nonsense? But when Hitler became chancellor, well-wishing friends advised my parents to leave Germany.

So my father took leave of his beloved homeland, where he was born and raised, and for which he had fought in the First World War. Mother and I followed shortly, and we were reunited in Strasbourg, just over the French border. We took with us only a few of our possessions. It was the end of our normal, accustomed way of life; we had become homeless, wandering Jews, without a nationality and without rights.

For me, a curious three-year-old, it was an exciting time. I quickly learned new customs, a new language, and I made new friends. But a year later we had to move again; as German refugees, we were considered a security risk in border areas. We went to a village in the Vosges – another change. My parents had to learn new trades and a new language, to adapt to a very different culture, to do without most of the comforts of their previous lifestyle – and before that, to make a living under difficult circumstances...

A year later, the factory that employed my mother burned down, which necessitated another move, this time to Marseille. Again my parents tried to eke out a living, and they built up a rather precarious existence. We frequently changed apartments, which meant I frequently had to change schools and friends. I never had the chance to form lasting relationships...

Then the Second World War broke out, and everything went to pieces. I was a stranger again, and an alien one on top of that...France was invaded and then occupied by the German army, and soon the Gestapo were making arrests...Our apartment and my parents' business were confiscated but, with the help of French friends, we went into hiding.

Finally my parents decided that our only hope of survival lay in escaping over the Pyrenees to Spain. After walking for three days through snow-covered mountains, the Spanish *Guardia Civil* (border police) caught up with us. Luckily they let us through – as they did most of the nearly 10,000 Jews who illegally crossed into Spain. Had we been shipped back to France, it would have meant sure death...

As it was, we were torn apart at the Gerona police station. Father was sent to a camp in Miranda-del-Ebro, and mother to the local prison. I was left behind on my own. I spent the most miserable night of my life alone in a freezing cell, thinking I had lost my parents forever. The next day I landed in Gerona's orphanage, which did little to improve my spirits. There I turned thirteen (the age Jewish boys are received into the congregation of the faithful) – and missed my *bar-mitzvah*...

After a few months I was sent to join my mother, and together we were transferred to a prison in Madrid. Later the whole family was reunited, and in 1944, with the assistance of the Jewish Joint Welfare Committee, we were able to move to Palestine.

In spite of all the suffering the Germans caused my family and my people, I still feel attached to their history and culture, which I absorbed through my parents. I have done my best to recreate links with decent Germans. Still, I can never forget the six million Jews – including 1.5 million innocent children – who were tortured and exterminated by the Nazis and their helpers.

If forgiving means renouncing blind hatred and feelings of revenge – yes, then it is possible. I forgive those who stood by helplessly, and those who did not dare to speak up. I know how much courage it takes to stand up to authority and to oppose the kind of terror the Nazis imposed. But what about the monsters who committed the worst atrocities in human memory?

Is it possible to forgive Hitler and his henchmen, his SS commanders and soldiers, his death-camp guards, his Gestapo officials? Is it possible to forgive torturers and murderers who starved, machine-gunned, and gassed hundreds of thousands of helpless men, women, and children? Are there no limits to forgiveness?

David's question is, I think, not motivated by resentment toward the exterminators of his people, but by a fear that forgiving them would somehow spell exoneration. As someone committed to doing what he can to ensure that similar atrocities never happen again, he cannot bring himself to release them of their responsibility and guilt.

And he shouldn't. Who could ever take it upon himself to excuse a man like Hitler? But forgiveness is not about excusing or exonerating people, nor is it about weighing the morality – or immorality – of their actions.

Writing in 1947, when the full horrors of the Holocaust had only just come to light, C. S. Lewis wrote, "There is all the difference in the world between forgiving and excusing." Most people, he suggested, don't like to admit when they've done something wrong, so they make excuses for their actions. (In relation to Nazi atrocities, thousands of Germans claimed, after the fall of the Third Reich, that they were only following orders.) Instead of asking for forgiveness, people often try to get others to accept extenuating circumstances, and to see that they themselves aren't really at fault. But, Lewis continued, "if one is not really to blame, then there is nothing to forgive. In that sense forgiveness and excusing are almost opposites."

> Real forgiveness means looking steadily at the sin, the sin that is left over without any excuse, after all allowances have been made, and seeing it in all its horror, dirt, meanness and malice, and nevertheless being wholly reconciled to the person who has done it. That, and only that, is forgiveness.

While witnessing the beating of a young man by sheriff's deputies from the Los Angeles Police Department, Roberto Rodriguez decided to photograph them. Before he knew it, he was attacked by the same club-wielding officers. Hospitalised with a cracked skull, he was then jailed and charged with attempting to kill the officers who almost took his life.

Roberto, now a nationally syndicated columnist, fought back, and after seven long years, he won both an acquittal and a federal civil rights lawsuit. In the meantime, however, his attempts to challenge the system made him a marked man:

> Once during this time I was handcuffed to a bench in a police station, with my picture posted over me, and an article detailing my legal battle with the police department. Each officer who passed by was told not to forget who I was. Apparently they didn't, because during the next few years I was continually harassed – and arrested about sixty times.

Ask Roberto what he thinks about forgiving, and he has answers. But he has plenty of questions, too.

> You ask me about forgiveness? Do I need to forgive the deputies who beat me, who made me believe – in the middle of the night – that they were driving me to my final destination? Do I need to forgive the officers who falsely arrested me and relentlessly pursued me, the district attorney who filed charges against me, the prosecutors who tried to put me away? Do I need to forgive the politicians who wouldn't touch me with a ten-foot pole when I pleaded with them for help, or the reporters who painted me as a criminal? And what about my own lawyer, who abandoned my case two days before trial?

I realize that we cannot be fully human if we have hatred within us – if we are consumed by anger or harbour
resentment. These emotions define our lives. Especially
for someone who has been brutalised and dehumanised,
getting rid of these debilitating emotions is fundamental
to healing. But doing that also means searching for something else to fill the void: searching for what it actually
means to be human.

I began that search in 1998, on my birthday, when I
sang for the first time in almost thirty years. A few months
later, I started to paint, and then to write fiction. I had
finally begun to regain my humanity.

I still haven't completely recovered from my trauma,
but at least I can smile, laugh, and love life once again, and
I can make others laugh and smile. I sing at nursing homes
and senior centres. I arrived at this through my pursuit of
justice, though also through prayer and meditation.

Though thousands of people of colour suffer mistreatment
at the hands of the law each year, most are not so fortunate
as Roberto. Most never see justice served. Should they too
be expected to forgive their oppressors? Roberto thinks
they must, and not only for their own sake:

> Because these abuses continue year after year, there is a lot
> of bitterness on America's streets, especially among those
> who have been brutalised and falsely imprisoned. Some
> are zombies. Others are walking time-bombs, filled with
> hate and ready to explode. And they do explode. Look
> what happened in Los Angeles in 1992, after the Rodney

Roberto Rodriguez

King verdict. Tragically, such outrage usually hurts the very people it is supposed to avenge: family, friends and neighbours.

All this is not a personal tragedy, but a societal one. It is like an out-of-control disease. Far from being a cure, forgiveness is in this realm a luxury at best. Yet precisely because there continue to be such gross injustices, those who have been dehumanised need to forgive – to heal on their own, without waiting for apologies. Forgiveness does not require apologies.

Of course this does not mean simply folding one's arms and going merrily home, oblivious of ongoing injustices. It simply means that as one struggles to regain one's humanity and fights for one's rights, one can do so without anger, hatred, and bitterness.

To be more specific: forgiving someone who has brutalised you may help them toward becoming more human. But it is only part of the solution. As a society, we have learned that people who commit acts of violence such as torturing or killing others need more than forgiveness if they are to be prevented from committing similar crimes again. They need treatment. An oppressor will never find true peace until he exorcises his own demons.

After Louisiana businessman Bill Chadwick lost his son, Michael, to a drunk driver, he "wanted to see justice done." Like Roberto, however, he discovered that justice alone couldn't bring him the closure he was looking for.

My twenty-one-year-old son Michael was killed instantly on October 23, 1993, in a car crash. His best friend, who was in the back seat, was also killed. The driver, who had been drinking heavily and was speeding recklessly, received minor injuries; he was subsequently charged with two counts of vehicular homicide. Michael had only a trace of alcohol in his system, and his best friend had none.

The wheels of justice grind very slowly. The courts took more than a year to find the case against the driver. We attended hearing after hearing, and each time the case was delayed. There was even an attempt by the defence attorney to discredit the findings of the blood-alcohol tests, although this was unsuccessful. Finally, the defendant pleaded guilty and was sentenced to six years per count, to be served concurrently.

We suggested to the probation office that a boot camp-style programme might be of benefit to him – we really weren't out to hurt him, but we believed he needed to pay for what he had done. All the same, we received a pretty ugly letter from his mother suggesting that we had somehow pushed for the maximum sentence. She said that if it had been her son who died, with Michael driving, she would not have held a grudge. I suggested that until her son were actually dead, she should not talk about what she

Bill and Michael Chadwick

would or wouldn't do.

Her son was finally sentenced to six months in boot camp, with the rest of his six-year sentence to be served on intensive parole. In six months, her son was coming home. Ours was not.

I guess I had bought into the belief that, somehow, things would be different after the driver had been brought to justice. I think that is what people mean when they talk about "closure." We think that if there is someone to blame, then we can put the matter to rest; because then the victim will get some sort of justice, and the pain will finally go away. In the years since Michael's death, I have read countless accounts of bereaved people who are looking for closure of this sort. I have also seen them on The Oprah Winfrey Show, shouting for the death penalty, as if having the perpetrator dead would somehow help.

I was angry at the driver, of course. But I was angry at Michael, too. After all, he had made some really bad decisions that night; he had put his life in jeopardy. I had to go through this anger in order to come to grips with my feelings. However, even after the sentencing, I did not find closure. What I did find was a big hole in my soul – and nothing to fill it with.

It was some months later that it hit me: until I could forgive the driver, I would never find the closure I was looking for. Forgiving was different from removing responsibility. The driver was still responsible for Michael's death, but I had to forgive him before I could let the incident go. No amount of punishment could ever even the score. I had to be willing to forgive without the score being even. And this process of forgiveness did not really involve the driver – it involved me. It was a process that I had to go through; I had to change, no matter what he did.

The road to forgiveness was long and painful. I had to forgive more than just the driver. I had to forgive Michael, and God (for allowing it to happen), and myself. Ultimately, it was forgiving myself that was the most difficult. There were many times in my own life I had driven Michael places when I myself was under the influence of alcohol. That was a hard recognition – my need to forgive myself. My anger at other people was just my own fear turned outward. I had projected my own guilt onto others – the driver, the courts, God, Michael – so that I would not have to look at myself. And it wasn't until I could see my part in this that my outlook could change.

> This is what I learned: that the closure we seek comes in forgiving. And this closure is really up to us, because the power to forgive does not lie outside us, but within.

In a society like ours, where victim's rights are increasingly seen as unassailable, Bill's insights are not popular ones. For many people, even vindication by a court is no longer enough. They want a personal role in the act of retribution. In several states, murder victims' families are offered spots in the witness rooms of execution chambers, or the opportunity to make statements at sentencing.

Not long ago I read that at the sentencing of Kip Kinkel, a fifteen-year-old who went on a shooting spree in Springfield, Oregon, in 1998, family members of his victims grew so angry that the judge had to cut them off and call the court to order. At one especially chilling moment, the mother of one victim spoke of her agony, and said with unabashed relish that she hoped Kip would be tortured by it in the same way she was for the rest of his life. "That, for me, is the ultimate justice."

However justified this woman's quest might seem, it is a fruitless one. Blinded by her grief, and determined to make the person responsible for it share it with her, she is seeking solace in a place she will never find it: revenge. Though my heart goes out to her, it is clear to me that she will never find healing, but only further heartache and deep disillusionment.

Mary Foley a British woman who also lost a child to teen violence, is on a very different quest. In April 2005, after an argument at a birthday party, her fifteen-year-old daughter Charlotte was stabbed to death by another girl.

Charlotte was so excited about going to that party. It was a sweet sixteen thing, and she knew some of the girls who were going to be there, so I never really thought much about it. She did her hair and her eyebrows – all that stuff – and off she went.

Around 1 a.m. the phone woke me up. It was one of Charlotte's friends, and she was totally distraught. She said, "Charlotte's been stabbed, she's in the hospital." Then the phone went dead...

At the hospital, I was led to a room. A nurse and two doctors came in. The nurse said simply, "I'm so sorry, but Charlotte's dead." I just couldn't believe it was true. There was no way I could begin to take in the fact she was gone. I hadn't even had a chance to say goodbye.

The following day, we went to identify her body. I stared at her – a sheet covered her, up to her neck and she still looked alive, just lying there so peacefully. I prayed that some miracle would happen and she would start breathing.

Meanwhile, we learned what had happened, in bits and pieces. Charlotte knew this girl Marisha, who knew Beatriz, and apparently Marisha and Beatriz had an on-going feud. It wasn't just an argument: Marisha had threatened to shank Beatriz, and so on. They'd argued on the phone that same evening, and were planning to have it out later that night, at the party. My daughter knew nothing of this...

At any rate, around midnight Charlotte and Beatriz exchanged words on the dance floor. Shortly after that, Charlotte went upstairs to freshen up. As she came out of the bedroom onto the landing, Beatriz said, "What did you say to me downstairs?" and stabbed her with a 4-inch kitchen knife. She had brought two knives in her handbag. My daughter bled to death.

As Mary sat and sobbed through the subsequent trial in London's famed Old Bailey, she at first seethed with anger and disbelief. Gradually, however, she felt her rage ebbing away, and eventually she felt a strange sense of compassion for Beatriz. By the end of the proceedings, her overriding desire was to forgive the girl and offer her the maternal guidance she had never had.

Forgiveness did not come immediately, even after I knew it was what I wanted. It was *hard*. My main struggle was seeing Charlotte being stabbed in my imagination, and knowing that I hadn't been there to help her. I often envisaged her bleeding to death. When I saw these things in my mind, the old anger would begin to rise up again in me, and I had to remind myself why I had chosen to forgive: so that I could release all that pain and hurt into the hands of God.

In March 2006, Beatriz was convicted of murder and sentenced to fourteen years to life. Asked if her decision to forgive Beatriz means that she disagrees with the severity of her punishment, Mary demurs. In fact, she hopes that the sentence will send out a strong message to other young people who carry knives. She notes that the girl had a history of violence and had drawn up a hit list of eighteen people. But as a devout Christian, she also admits feeling that the longest sentence will not necessarily change a criminal's heart. "What Beatriz needs most is a living relationship with Jesus. In the end, that's the only thing in the world that can change her." And so she refuses to simply write off her daughter's murderer:

> Beatriz's background is so, so sad. It doesn't condone what she did to my daughter. But she has had so many challenges in her life. She's had trouble at school, at home, with boyfriends, and with girlfriends. All sorts of stuff has happened to her. Her father is wanted by police in connection with the attempted murder of her mother. At one point she was found homeless. She thinks she's worthless. Worst of all, there's never been anyone there for her to talk to. What I am trying to do is fill that gap in her life and be the person who believes she has something positive to offer. In a way, I feel maternal towards her. Maybe because I'm Charlotte's mum I can influence her to learn something while she's in prison.

Today Mary is a popular speaker in schools throughout London. In retelling her story, she draws connections between unhealthy friendships and the violent incidents they often lead to, and she talks about the links between forgiveness and nonviolent conflict resolution. Sometimes, she shares a letter Beatriz sent her from prison:

Dear Mrs. Foley,

It's Beatriz. I don't have the words to say to make it all better and I know nothing I say won't change the situation but I need you to know just how sorry I am for doing what I did. Charlotte should be here and I really regret that split-second of madness. I should never have done that. It was a nasty thing to do and I'm sorry for the pain and the grief I have caused you and your younger children. I'm really sorry Mrs. Foley for hurting your little girl. I didn't mean to take her life. I really didn't. Those were never my intentions. I didn't even mean to stab Charlotte. I can't answer why I took it to that extent. Even at court, I got no reply to why I went over the top. I don't know, Mrs. Foley, what made me extend my arm towards Charlotte, causing all this pain to so many people, but I know how much I wish I could reverse the past. I'm really sorry, Mrs. Foley. I'm sorry to Charlotte as well. She should be here. There's nothing more I can say but sorry, Mrs. Foley. I wish there was more I could do to prove how sorry I am. I'm so upset about all this. All this drama was too unnecessary. Please don't be sad, Mrs. Foley. I hope you don't mind me writing to you. I hope you can find happiness again one

Mary Foley

day. I hate being the person who made you so sad and upset. I feel horrible for what I did to Charlotte. It was so unfair. I didn't want none of this to happen. I really didn't. I'm sorry, Mrs. Foley. It's hard to find the words to say to someone you've hurt, but I just needed you to know how sorry I am. I understand if you don't reply but I would love to hear from you. It'd mean a lot to me. I didn't mean to hurt your daughter, Mrs. Foley.

Lots of love from Beatriz.

P.S. I'd do anything to bring your Charlotte back.

Asked about her reaction to Beatriz's letter, Mary's thoughts involuntarily fly to the P.S. "Well, there *isn't* anything she can do to bring Charlotte back." But Mary adds that receiving the letter (and a few more since then) have helped her to "remember that Beatriz is a human, a young person, with emotions."

As for the rest of the family, Mary says each of them is in a different place as regards coming to terms with Charlotte's death. Of her son, Dion, for example, she says that he "hasn't even thought about forgiveness," whereas her husband, Paul, has chosen to forgive. From Mary again:

> Most of my extended family and friends think I'm crazy! I feel they want to say it, but don't, because they don't want to hurt my feelings. They may not criticize me to my face, or even verbalise their discomfort, but you can hear it in the questions they ask me. In the end, though, all the criticism in the world won't stop me. What motivates me – what gets me out of bed in the morning – is knowing that God has a purpose for my life. In spite of what I've gone through, I believe that God will use this tragedy for his glory. When I share my story and see the light switch on in people's lives, so that they see that they can choose to forgive – that's what motivates me. They see that they don't have to be reined in or held down by bitterness for the rest of their lives.

The Deeds of Mercy

Though justice be thy plea, consider this:
that in the course of justice none of us
should see salvation. We do pray for mercy,
and that same prayer doth teach us all
to render the deeds of mercy.

WILLIAM SHAKESPEARE

In his novel *Too Late the Phalarope,* Alan Paton writes of a respected man who commits what his society sees as an unpardonable sin: adultery. When the affair is brought to light, the man's family is devastated. His friends leave him, his relatives spurn him, and his father dies in shame. Yet a neighbour agonises over the incident: "An offender can be punished," he says. "But to punish and not to restore, that is the greatest of all offences... If a man takes unto himself God's right to punish, then he must also take upon himself God's promise to restore."

If there is anything that reveals the apparent contradictions of the mystery we call forgiveness, it is this thorny "offence." Most of us find it difficult to let go even of relatively small grudges, yet restoration or reconciliation – call it what you will – demands not only that, but the active attempt to embrace a person whom it would be far easier to avoid.

When Miami native Chris Carrier was ten, a former family employee abducted him, assaulted him, shot him in the head, and left him to die in the Florida Everglades. But that isn't the end of the story:

> Friday, December 20, 1974, was no ordinary day. It was the last day of school before the Christmas holidays, and we got out early.
>
> I stepped off the bus at 1:15 p.m. and began to walk home. An older-looking man who happened to be walking towards me on the sidewalk appeared to recognise me. Just two houses away from home, he introduced himself as a friend of my father. He told me he was hosting a party for my father and asked if I would help him with some decorations.
>
> I agreed and walked back up the street with him to the local youth centre where he had parked his motor caravan. Once inside the vehicle, I put down my things and made myself comfortable.

Chris Carrier

The Miami I knew quickly disappeared as he drove north. In an area removed from suburban traffic, he stopped on the side of the road. He claimed that he had missed a turn. He handed me a map, instructing me to look for a certain number, and went into the back of the motor caravan "to get something."

As I studied the map and waited, I felt a quick sting in the shoulder, and then another. I turned around to see him standing behind me with an ice pick in his hand. Then he pulled me out of my seat and onto the floor. Kneeling over me, he stabbed me in the chest several times. I pleaded with him to stop and promised him that if he would let me go, I wouldn't say anything.

I was immeasurably relieved when he stood up. He told me that he was going to drop me off somewhere, after which he would call my father and let him know where I was. He allowed me to sit in the back of the motor caravan as he drove. Yet I was painfully aware that this situation was beyond my control. When I asked him why he was doing this to me, he said that my father had "cost him a great deal of money."

After driving for another hour or so, he turned onto a dusty side road. He told me this was where my father would pick me up. We walked out together into the bushes and I sat down where he told me I should sit. The last thing I remembered was him walking away.

Six days later, the evening of December 26, Chris was found by a local deer hunter. His head was bloody and his eyes were black. He had been shot through the head. Miraculously, there was no brain damage, but he didn't remember being shot.

In the years that followed, Chris struggled daily with the insecurity of knowing that his abductor was still at large.

Everywhere I went, the fear of what was around the corner, what was lurking in the shadows, haunted me. I was alarmed by every noise and motion. Was that a dog? What was that – is it really just the wind? What was that creak in the next room? Was someone coming in our back door? For three years I spent every night without fail in a sleeping bag at the foot of my parents' bed.

Chris also had to come to terms with the physical limitations caused by his injuries: he was now blind in one eye and could no longer take part in contact sports. And as any teenager would, he worried about his appearance.

Chris resented public mention of his survival, and remembers wondering how this "miracle" could have left him so miserable. Then, at the age of thirteen, he underwent a change, and began to see his nightmare differently. He realised his injuries could have been much worse – in fact, he could have died. He also recognised that staying angry would never change anything. He decided to stop feeling sorry for himself, and to get on with his life instead.

Then, on September 3, 1996, Chris received a telephone call that changed his life once again. It was a detective from the Coral Gables police department, and he was calling to notify him that an elderly man at a local nursing home, David McAllister, had confessed to being his abductor. (He was, though in the eyes of the law there was never enough evidence to bring him to trial.) David had worked as an aide for an elderly uncle in the Carrier family, but had been fired on account of his drinking problems. Chris visited David the following day.

> It was an awkward moment, walking into his room, but as soon as I saw him I was overwhelmed with compassion. The man I found was not an intimidating kidnapper, but a frail seventy-seven-year-old who had been blind for the last half-dozen years.
>
> David's body was ruined by alcoholism and smoking – he weighed little more than sixty pounds. He had no family, or if he did, they wanted nothing to do with him, and no friends. The only material possessions he had were some pictures that children in a nearby primary school had drawn for him. David had a roommate, but they

didn't even know each other or communicate. Here was a man who faced death with only his regrets to keep him company.

When I first spoke to David, he was rather callous. I suppose he thought I was a police officer. A friend who had accompanied me wisely asked him a few simple questions that led to him admitting that he had abducted me. He then asked, "Did you ever wish you could tell that young boy that you were sorry for what you did?" David answered emphatically, "I wish I could." That was when I introduced myself to him.

Unable to see, David clasped my hand and told me he was sorry for what he had done to me. As he did, I looked down at him, and it came over me like a wave: Why should anyone have to face death without family, friends, the joy of life – without hope? I couldn't do anything but offer him my forgiveness and friendship.

In the days that followed this dramatic meeting, Chris began to visit David as often as he could, usually bringing along his wife, Leslie, and their two daughters. The two men spent hours talking, reading, and even praying together, and as they did, the old man's hardness gradually melted away.

Throughout that week I shared with him about the victories of my recovery, and about my life since the horrifying day he had tried to kill me. I'd graduated from high school, from college, and then from graduate school. I had married; I had a beautiful wife and family. I shared these things with him so that he could understand, in the way the ancient Israelite Joseph tried to get his brothers to understand, after they had abandoned him, "That which you intended for evil, God has used for good." I let him know that he had not ruined my life, in the end, and that there was nothing between us now.

Three weeks later, just hours after Chris had tucked his ailing friend into bed for the night, David died.

Chris says it wasn't hard for him to forgive, though the reporters who later took interest in his story still don't understand how or why he did it. They admire his ability to forgive, but cannot understand what compelled him. They always go blank when the subject of forgiveness comes up, he says, and seem more comfortable focusing on the drama of his abduction and the details of his torture. But Chris knows why he forgave David:

> There is a very pragmatic reason for forgiving. When we are wronged, we can either respond by seeking revenge, or we can forgive. If we choose revenge, our lives will be consumed by anger. When vengeance is served, it leaves one empty. Anger is a hard urge to satisfy and can become habitual. But forgiveness allows us to move on.
>
> There is also a more compelling reason to forgive. Forgiveness is a gift – it is mercy. It is a gift that I have received and also given away. In both cases, it has been completely satisfying.

When infamous "pick-axe murderer" Karla Faye Tucker was executed on February 3, 1998, in Huntsville, Texas, small clusters of death penalty protesters held a candle-light vigil. But many more of the hundreds gathered outside the prison were there to cheer her death. A cardboard sign waved by one man said it all: "May heaven help you. It's sure as hell we won't!"

Inside the prison, however, a man named Ron Carlson was praying for Karla – not in the witness room for her vic-tims' families, where he could have been, but in the one set aside for the family of the murderer.

It has been two years since I met Ron and heard his re-markable journey from hatred to reconciliation, but what he told me sticks in my mind as if it were yesterday:

> Shortly after I came home one day at five after a hard day's work – it was the 13th of July, 1983 – the phone rang. It was my father. He said, "Ronnie, you need to come over to the shop right away. We have reason to believe your sister has been murdered." I was floored. I couldn't believe it. I couldn't even believe it when I saw her body being carried out of an apartment on television.
>
> Deborah was my sister, and she raised me. My mother and father divorced when I was very young, and my mother died when I was six. I had no brothers – just one sister – so Deborah was very special. *Very* special.
>
> Deborah made sure I had clothes to wear, and that there was food on the table. She helped me do my home-

Karla Faye Tucker

work, and slapped me on the hand when I did something wrong. She became my mother.

Now she was dead, with dozens of puncture wounds all over her body, and the pick-axe that made them had been left in her heart. Deborah was not one to have enemies. She had simply been in the wrong place at the wrong time. The murderers had come over to steal motorcycle parts from the house where she was staying, and when they discovered Jerry Dean – the guy she was with – they hacked him to death. They were high on drugs. Then they discovered Deborah, so they had to kill her too...

Houston was in an uproar. Headlines screamed the gory details of the crime, and the entire city lived in fear. A few weeks later the murderers – two drug addicts named Karla Faye Tucker and Daniel Ryan Garret – were turned in by relatives. Subsequently tried and convicted, they were both sentenced to death by lethal injection. (Daniel later died in prison.) Still, Ron felt no relief.

I was glad they were caught, of course, but I wanted to kill them myself. I was filled with sheer hatred, and I wanted to get even. I wanted to bury that pick-axe in Karla's heart, just like she had buried it in my sister's.

Ron says that he was a problem drinker and drug abuser before his sister's death, but that after he buried her, he became more heavily involved than ever. Then, about a year later, his father was shot to death.

I was often drunk, and I'd get high on LSD, marijuana, whatever I could get my hands on, as often as I could. I also got into a lot of fights with my wife. I was very angry. I even wanted to kill myself...

Then one night, I just couldn't take it any more. I guess I had come to the point where I knew I had to do something about the hatred and rage that was building in me. It was getting so bad that all I wanted to do was destroy things and kill people. I was heading down the same path as the people who had killed my sister and my dad. Anyway, I opened a Bible, and began to read.

It was really weird. I was high – I was smoking doobies and reading the word of God! But when I got to where they crucified Jesus, I slammed the book shut. For some reason it struck me like it never had before: My God, they even killed Jesus!

Then I got down on my knees – I'd never done this before – and asked God to come into my life and make me into the type of person he wanted me to be, and to be the Lord of my life. That's basically what happened that night.

Later I read more, and a line from the Lord's Prayer – this line that says "forgive us as we forgive" – jumped out at me.

The meaning seemed clear: "You won't be forgiven until you forgive." I remember arguing to myself, "I can't do that, I could never do that," and God seemed to answer right back, "Well, Ron, *you* can't. But through me you can."

Not long after that I was talking on the phone with a friend, and he asked me if I knew that Karla was in town, at the Harris County Jail. "You ought to go down there and give her a piece of your mind," he said. Now this friend didn't know where I'd been going spiritually, and I didn't tell him. But I did decide to go see Karla.

When I got there, I walked up to her and told her that I was Deborah's brother. I didn't say anything else at first. She looked at me and said, "You are *who?*" I repeated myself, and she still stared, like she just couldn't believe what she was hearing. Then she started to cry.

I said, "Karla, whatever comes out of all this, I want you to know that I forgive you, and that I don't hold anything against you." At that point all my hatred and anger was taken away. It was like some great weight had been lifted off my shoulders.

Ron says he talked with Karla at length, and that during their discussion he discovered that she, too, had recently come to believe in God, and that her faith had changed her whole outlook on life. It was then that he decided he would have to return and find out more about her:

At first I had just wanted to go in, forgive her, and move on, but after that first visit I needed to go back. I wanted to find out if she was really sincere about this Christian walk she claimed to be on. I also wanted to find out why people kill, why they murder each other. I never found that out, but I did find out that Karla was real. I also found out, through her, that people *can* change and that God is real.

Karla's mother had been a prostitute and a drug addict, and she'd introduced her daughter to all that when she was very young. Karla started shooting drugs when she was ten. It was only in prison that she turned her life around – through a ministry at the Harris County Jail that reached out to the women, gave them free Bibles, and helped them find something to live for.

Ron visited Karla on death row every second month or so for the next two years, and he also wrote letters to her. They were soon close friends. He remembers:

People just couldn't understand it. They said something was obviously wrong with me – that I should hate the person who killed Deborah, not reach out to her. One relative told me I was disgracing my sister's memory, the way I was acting, and that she was probably rolling in her grave. Another made a public statement the day Karla was to be executed about how happy he and his family were to know that she would soon be dead. He said, "We have a saying in Texas – 'What goes around, comes around.'"

Karla herself was mystified by Ron's attitude toward her. Talking with a Dutch television crew who interviewed her shortly before her execution, she said: "It's unbelievable.

Amazing. Forgiveness is one thing. But to go beyond that and reach out to me – to actively love me...?" If anything, she found it easier to understand the thousands of Texans who wanted her dead:

> I can understand their rage. Who wouldn't? It's an expression of their hurt and pain. And I know people don't think I deserve forgiveness. But who *does* deserve it? I've been given a new life, and the hope – the promise – that this is not the final reality.

Karla went to her death bravely, smiling as she made her last statement – "I am so sorry...I hope God gives you all peace through this" – and humming as she was strapped to the gurney and pumped with lethal chemicals.

As for Ron, he insists that it was useless to execute her: "It does no good whatsoever to kill anyone. It does not make our streets safer. It just makes more victims. Sure, I miss my sister. But I miss Karla too."

When Reconciling Is Impossible

> It may be infinitely worse to refuse to forgive than to murder, because the latter may be an impulse of a moment of heat, whereas the former is a cold and deliberate choice of the heart.
>
> GEORGE MACDONALD

When her seven-year-old daughter was kidnapped from their tent during a camping trip in Montana, Marietta Jaeger's initial reaction was one of rage:

> I was seething with hate, ravaged with a desire for revenge. "Even if Susie were brought back alive and well this minute, I could kill that man," I said to my husband, and I meant it with every fibre of my being.

Justifiable as her reaction was, Marietta says she soon realised that no amount of anger could bring her daughter back. Not that she was ready to forgive her daughter's

Marietta and Susie Jaeger

kidnapper: she told herself that to do that would be to betray her daughter. Yet deep down inside, she sensed that forgiving him was the only way she would ever be able to cope with her loss.

It was that sense – that and sheer desperation – that led her to pray not only for her daughter's safe return, but for her kidnapper as well. As she prayed over weeks, and then months, her prayers became easier and more earnest. She simply had to find the person who had taken away her beloved child. And she even felt an uncanny desire to talk with him face to face.

Then one night, a year to the minute after her daughter had been abducted, Marietta received a phone call. It was the kidnapper. Marietta was afraid – the voice was smug and taunting – but she was also surprised at her strange but genuine feeling of compassion for the man at the other end of the line. And she noticed that, as she calmed down, he did too. They talked for over an hour.

Luckily Marietta was able to record their conversation. Even so it was months before the FBI finally tracked him down and arrested him, and it was only then that she knew her daughter would never come home. The investigators had found the backbone of a small child among the kidnapper's belongings.

State law offered the death penalty, but Marietta was not out for revenge. She writes: "By then, I had finally come to learn that true justice is not about punishment, but restoration and rehabilitation." Later she requested that her child's killer be given an alternative sentence of life imprisonment with psychiatric counselling. The tormented young man soon committed suicide, but she never regretted her decision to offer him help. And her efforts at peacemaking did not end there. Today, she is part of a group that works for reconciliation between murderers and the families of victims.

Kelly, a long-time acquaintance, lost her fiancé when he left her ten days before their wedding date. It was the last time she ever saw him. They had been engaged for more than a year, and although the relationship had occasionally faltered, she was sure that this time everything was going to work out. She was deeply in love, and very excited. She had finally graduated from nursing school, and her wedding dress was nearly finished. Then everything fell apart:

My fiancé revealed that he had been dishonest with me – there were things in his past that were still an obstacle to our marriage. To make things worse, he wanted to run away from it all rather than confront it. I was shattered. I wept for days and was heartbroken for years. I blamed myself for his dishonesty, and I became bitter.

Thirty years later, Kelly is still single, but she is no longer bitter. Even though she cannot tell him, she has genuinely and entirely forgiven her fiancé. And although she sometimes still aches for the marriage that never was and the love she lost, she has found fulfilment of another kind in helping and serving other people – the old and the sick, expectant mothers, and disabled children. Happy and energetic, she is too busy to entertain self-pity, and few, if any, of her friends know about her past:

> Because I am single, I can do things a busy wife and mother could never do. I can give of myself whenever and wherever I am needed. And I have cared for and loved more children than I ever could have otherwise. But before I could do any of this, I had to stop focusing on myself and my loss. First I had to forgive.

When Julie discovered that her husband, Mike, was molesting their daughter, she was beside herself with shock and anger. Yet after confronting him and taking steps to ensure that his behaviour would not continue, she decided to stay with him. For one thing, she wanted to believe him when he insisted it would never happen again; for another, she could not bear the thought of asking him to leave. But the family broke up anyway.

I was foundering on the verge of desperation. Mike had become a stranger to me, and I could no longer live with him in what had become a hell. We stayed together about a year, struggling to rebuild our relationship – or at very least keep it from falling any further apart – but it was no use.

Finally I left Mike and moved back to my old hometown, taking the children with me. I was angry, hurt, hateful, rejected, despairing, outraged, humiliated – and even this long string of adjectives cannot express what I felt. A battle raged in my heart.

Part of me wanted to forgive Mike, but another part wanted to lash out at him in revenge. This was especially so after he divorced me and married again. Every time I thought of his new wife it rekindled my anger.

This was my battle: deep down, I felt I should forgive Mike, and I genuinely wanted to. But how should I express my forgiveness practically? And how could I, when he showed so little remorse?

I didn't want to gloss over what he had done in any way, and I had let him know, when I left him, that I could never allow our children to stay with him again. But aside from that there seemed nothing I could do, other than acknowledge the fact that our marriage was over for good, and accept the divorce.

It has not been an easy battle, and it continues still, as I witness the effect of the abuse and the breakup on our five children. I have also discovered that forgiveness is not a one-time thing – it must be affirmed again and again. Sometimes I doubt that I have ever forgiven Mike at all, and I have to battle through that, too. But I know that, ultimately, the wrongs he did to me cannot destroy me.

Anne Coleman, the woman whose story I told in the first chapter, came to a similar conclusion after the murder of her daughter, Frances, and the subsequent death of her son, Daniel, who could not cope with his sister's death. Though this double tragedy shattered every semblance of "normal" life for their mother, she was determined to stand strong, and not to concede defeat. Today, instead of nursing her own wounds, she tends to those of the people around her. In fact, she does much more than that in her work as a volunteer counsellor to the men on Delaware's death row.

Anne's involvement with prison inmates began after she met Barbara Lewis, a woman whose son had been sentenced to death. After going to see him together, they began to visit other inmates as well:

That's how I met Billy. He'd had no visitors, and he was very lonely. I cry when I think of how he was hanged; how they made him stand on the gallows in that howling wind for at least fifteen minutes while they waited for the witnesses to arrive. After his execution I thought I couldn't go on.

Then I got to know a little boy called Marcus. His father is also on death row. He has no mother and has lost both of his sisters, and he has nightmares because now he's going to lose his father, too...

I know that hating someone is not going to bring my daughter back. And at this point, I don't know if I'll ever find the person who killed her, anyway. But one has to find healing somehow, and I've found it by helping the Barbaras and Marcuses of this world. Helping them has given me more healing than I ever imagined.

On April 20, 1999, Brad and Misty Bernall of Littleton, Colorado, lost their daughter Cassie in a school shooting that left her and fourteen other classmates dead. Like Anne, the Bernalls may never fully come to terms with their daughter's death. In a way, such acceptance would be unnatural, because the memory of a child is something a parent wants to keep alive forever. Nor are they ready, yet, to say "I forgive" from the bottom of their hearts. Still, they are "working on it," as Misty says, rather than seeking revenge.

Brad and Misty Bernall with Cassie and Chris

Brad and Misty are frustrated by the knowledge that their daughter's killers might have been stopped, had parents, law enforcement officials and school administrators intervened earlier. Nevertheless, while many families of school shooting victims around the country have hired attorneys, filed lawsuits, and become embroiled in bitter shouting matches over who is to blame for their children's deaths, the Bernalls have resisted invitations to join the fray. As Misty put it in a book she wrote about her daughter about six months after her death:

Anger is a destructive emotion. It eats away at whatever peace you have, and in the end it causes nothing but greater pain than you began with. It also makes it that much harder for others to console you, when you're busy nursing resentment. It's not as if I don't have those seeds in me – I know I do – but I'm not going to let other people water them.

There's also the whole question of revenge. It's normal, I think, to want to bite back, whether through filing a lawsuit or by other means. But in the case of Cassie's murderers, we could never go after their families. Even if we did sue them and won, no amount of money is going to bring our daughter back.

Clearly, not every story has a tidy ending. Sometimes, as happened in Littleton, murderers kill themselves. Sometimes, as in the case of Anne's daughter, they are never caught. Fiancés (and even spouses) up and leave, never to be heard from again. Marietta tried to reach out to the man who kidnapped her daughter, and found him too tormented to be helped. Then there are those like Julie, who gather up their courage and confront the person they want to forgive, only to discover that he is not the least bit sorry for his actions. Anyone whose wounds are left to bleed in such painful ways is bound to remain affected for the rest of his or her life.

Unfortunately, those who take the most pains to demand an apology may find that it never comes; and those who smoulder year after year, burning with the desire to see justice finally served, may be similarly disappointed. The fuel of bitterness is always expended in vain. But the opposite is true, too. The love of a forgiving heart is never wasted. It can fill the deepest hole and heal the deepest wound.

Forgiving in Everyday Life

To love at all is to be vulnerable. The only place outside Heaven where you can be perfectly safe from all the dangers and perturbations of love is Hell.

C. S. LEWIS

Most of us will probably never be faced with forgiving a murderer or rapist. But all of us are faced daily with the need to forgive a partner, child, friend or colleague – perhaps dozens of times in a single day. And while doing the latter may be less difficult than the former, it is just as important. In his poem "A Poison Tree," William Blake shows how the smallest resentment can blossom and bear deadly fruit:

> I was angry with my friend:
> I told my wrath, my wrath did end.
> I was angry with my foe:
> I told it not, my wrath did grow.

And I watered it in fears,
Night and morning with my tears;
And I sunned it with smiles,
And with soft deceitful wiles.

And it grew both day and night,
Till it bore an apple bright;
And my foe beheld it shine,
And he knew that it was mine,

And into my garden stole
When the night had veiled the pole:
In the morning glad I see
My foe outstretched beneath the tree.

The seeds of Blake's tree are the petty grudges of everyday life. Often they are so small that they are barely noticeable, at least at first. But even if we do not consciously tend to them, they will germinate over time. That is why it is so important to weed out even the most insignificant ones as soon as they take root in us – before they can grow.

I had to learn not to hold on to grudges early in my life. My childhood was a happy one for the most part, but I had my share of unpleasant experiences. A sickly child, I was diagnosed with hydrocephalus ("water on the brain") soon after I was born, and a doctor told my mother I would never walk. Even though this did not prove to be true – I started walking at two-and-a-half – classmates who found out about my condition began calling me "water head." Though this probably hurt my parents more than me, the nickname upset me a good deal too.

When I was six, I had to have a large tumour removed from my leg. This was the first of many such operations over the next three decades. The surgery lasted two hours, and the threat of infection – this was before the days of anti-biotics, and we lived in the backwoods of Paraguay – hung over me for days. After my leg was stitched shut, I had to walk home from the hospital: no one offered me crutches, let alone a wagon ride. I can still see my father's shocked face as I limped into our house, though he didn't say a thing.

That was typical of my parents. We never heard them speak ill of others, and they did not allow us to, either. Like any other parents, they struggled with their feelings when they felt that one of us children had been mistreated, whether by a teacher or any other adult. But they insisted that the only way to overcome the little indignities of life was to rise above them by forgiving.

When I was fourteen, we moved to the United States. The change from a village in the South American wilderness to a high school in New York was enormous. The English language was perhaps the biggest barrier for me, but there were other obstacles to fitting in: I felt awkward and clumsy, and on top of that I was naturally shy. In short, I had very little self-esteem.

Every child wants to be recognised by his peers, and I was no different. I desperately wanted to be accepted, and I went out of my way to please my new classmates. At first I was spurned, especially by the class bully. Then I began to fight back, taunting him by talking about him behind his back and laughing in his face when he tried to find out what I had said. Not surprisingly, I received my share of bloody noses.

In my twenties, I dealt with more damaging feelings of rejection, when the woman I was engaged to turned her back on me and broke off our relationship. It was a struggle for me to let go of my hurt feelings and forgive her, especially since I had no idea why she had ended the relationship. Later I convinced myself that it was my fault that things had gone wrong, because I was such an awkward misfit, and I had to forgive myself too.

A few years later, my hopes were dashed again, when another woman broke off our relationship after several months. My world crashed around me as I tried to make sense of what had happened. What had I done wrong?

That second time it took even longer to battle my emotions and rebuild my confidence. But my father assured me that in time I would find the right partner, and a few years down the road he proved to be right.

Perhaps the hardest thing about practicing forgiveness in daily life is that it requires us to confront the reality of our feelings toward those we know best. It is difficult enough to forgive a stranger we might never see again, but it is much harder to forgive a person we love and trust. Our family, our friends, the people we feel closest to at work – they not only know our strengths, but also our weaknesses, our frailties, and our quirks. And when they turn on us, we are often left reeling. At least that's what Clare Stober, a former business-woman who is now a member of my church, experienced:

> Before leaving the advertising agency I co-owned and moving to another state, I had to settle affairs with my partner of ten years. This was complicated by the fact that he and his wife had once been very close to me and had been fellow church members for the past fifteen years. Over time we had grown apart, and I felt I could no longer continue working with them.
>
> None of our advisors wanted to tell me how best to divide our assets equitably. I wanted to go beyond just being fair – I wanted nothing weighing on my conscience – so I made a proposal to that effect. I thought it was a very generous distribution. But my partner saw the whole thing differently and stopped talking to me the day I told him of my desire to leave the business. Unfortunately, it was two more months before I felt my tasks were sufficiently handed over, and the transition was long, silent, lonely, and punctuated by angry words.

We still had not signed an agreement by the time I left. Lawyers had been brought in by both sides, but they only clouded the waters. I had wanted an outside source to arbitrate the offer, but my partner fired the arbitrator and sought advice instead from an accountant we had worked with for seven years. The accountant quickly realised that his future lay with the partner who was continuing with the business and helped him to make my leaving very difficult.

It took a lot of offers and counter-offers to come to a final agreement. I won't go into details here, but the result of their demands was that I was made liable for one-half of the firm's earnings for the last full year I was with them, from January to December, even though I only received my share of the earnings through June. I ended up paying $50,000 in taxes which they should have paid.

When I realized what they had done, and that they had done it with forethought and deliberation, I was so angry I could not sleep for days. I felt they had conspired to crush me. I've been through a lot of difficult times in my life, but I have never spent so many sleepless nights, tossing and turning, consumed by anger and deep hurt. When I thought about what had happened during the day, the waves of anger that welled up within me were so powerful they would leave me shaking.

To make matters worse, a friend asked me, "What are you so upset about? It's only money." That made me even more angry. Sure it was "only money," and I didn't really need it at the time. But it was a *lot* of money, and it was mine, and they had cheated me. Obviously, the IRS could not be put off, though, so I wrote the cheque and hoped in a God of vengeance.

My journey to forgiveness took years. It was like crossing a stream by hopping from one stone to another. I took the first step as I was driving alone one night, listening to the radio, and a song came on about forgiveness. The performer explained the lyrics before he sang it. He talked about how we keep our hurts in a cupboard in our hearts and repeatedly bring them out to turn them over and replay them. We examine our hurts over and over, and nurse our self-pity.

There was a surprise at the end of the song: it talked about how we think we're imprisoning those who have hurt us by not forgiving them, but if we look at the face of the person locked in the tower, we'll see that it is our own. At that point I knew, at least intellectually, that forgiveness was the key to getting on with my life.

I took a second step when I began to examine my own feelings and realised that I was more hurt by my partner's cheating me out of money, than by his slander. It began to bother me that I had let money have such a hold on my life and feelings.

Another step came about a year later when I was embarking on a new chapter of my life in a new location. I was talking with a friend who knew my old partner, and she asked me if I had ever forgiven him. I quickly said, "Sure." She wasn't satisfied, but pressed further, explaining to me how important forgiveness was for both of our futures, even if we no longer worked together. She said that by not forgiving him, I was somehow binding him and not letting him get on with his life – not to mention that I was hurting my own future in the same way. I asked my friend, "So how does forgiveness work, then?" She described it as a gift – we can will to forgive as much as we want, but ultimately it must be given to us. Reluctantly, I began to will myself to forgive – though in retrospect I see that I still felt it was my partner who should be asking for forgiveness, not me.

The final step came later, during a time of deep spiritual introspection. I was trying to clear up everything in my life that had gone wrong up to that point, and make a clean slate before God. Frankly, I was getting nowhere – I thought I had nothing to clear up.

Then it hit me like a ton of bricks. Sure, I had been wronged, but I had done more than an equal share of wrongs in my life – against my partner, and against others. I sat down and wrote him a letter, telling him how much bitterness I had carried, and asking his forgiveness. I felt such a release as I licked that envelope and put the letter in the post. No matter what their answer, I could now be free of my anger.

About a month later, the same friend who had advised me to forgive happened to call me and asked me if I had been able to do so. I told her that I had, and that I now felt free. She answered, "I thought so. I've noticed a new freedom in him, too."

Already as a teenager, my father was known for his ability to listen and his tendency to think the best of people, and when he became a pastoral counsellor, these qualities stood him in good stead. Neither assertive nor articulate (he learned English only as an adult), he would rarely dispense advice, but take in a person's problems quietly and then offer a personal insight or an encouraging word.

Wherever Papa went, people wanted to talk to him. Many had things they wanted to get off their chests; others just needed a receptive ear. Whatever the case, they knew he would make time for them. Unfortunately, the very thing that drew people to him netted him the criticism of envious colleagues, who took advantage of his trust and turned on him.

Papa began to suffer from kidney problems around the time I was born, and as I grew up these problems became worse. Physically, life was harsh in the rural community where we lived: tropical diseases were rampant, and the infant mortality rate was very high. Added to that, there were tensions in our settlement, a close-knit intentional community that consisted primarily of immigrants who had fled wartime Europe.

Given these circumstances, the burden of Papa's responsibilities – he was an appointed leader of the community – weighed on him so heavily that it affected his health. At one point, after several weeks of steady physical decline,

The author's parents, Heinrich and Annemarie Arnold

his doctors even told him he had only forty hours to live. Fearing the worst, he summoned the entire community to his bedside and passed on his duties to three other men, one of them his brother-in-law.

As it turned out, Papa miraculously recovered, but rather than handing back his responsibilities to him, the community's new leaders told him that his working days were over: the doctor had declared him too weak to continue his demanding schedule.

In fact, the doctor had simply suggested a few weeks of rest. But the "misunderstanding" was deliberate – my father's colleagues wanted him out of the ministry. As ammunition for their case, they reminded him of the emotional instability he had displayed at the height of his illness, when he had seen strange things and had had bizarre dreams. What, they asked him, were they to make of all that? (Thirty years later another doctor discovered the reason for his hallucinations: they were a side-effect of the primitive bromide medications used to treat him.) Never the kind of person to fight back, Papa meekly gave in and took a new job in the local missionary hospital.

Not long after that, new problems surfaced. Worried that the community was moving away from its original basis – faith, mutual service, and brotherly love – and becoming a committee-led bureaucracy driven by rules and regulations, my parents joined a handful of other members in voicing their concerns. But they were not heard. Instead of welcoming their questions, the leadership accused them of trying to create a split, and several, including Papa, were excommunicated.

Papa was a skilled gardener – he had studied agriculture in Zurich – but even so he was unable to find work. As an outspoken opponent of Nazism, he was looked on with suspicion by the local Germans, who tended to be sympathetic toward Hitler. As for the British and American expatriates in the area, they feared him because he was German. Finally, he found employment as a farm manager in a leper colony.

In the early 1940s there was no cure for leprosy, and Papa was warned that if he accepted the position he might never see his wife or children again. (At that time the disease was thought to be contagious). But what could he do? He had to support himself somehow. He took the job.

Finally, after many months, Papa was permitted to rejoin the community. The day he returned I was so excited I could hardly stand it. As soon as I saw him I jumped into his arms. Then, riding on his shoulders as he walked toward our house, I called out to everyone we passed, "Papa is home!" Amazingly, my joy was met mostly with icy stares. It was only years later that I was able to understand. Yes, Papa had been allowed to come back. But he hadn't been forgiven.

Though the anguish my parents suffered in those years must have affected them both deeply, it never embittered them. In fact, it was only decades later that I found out about all that they had gone through – and not from them, but from friends. When I asked them why they hadn't stood up for themselves, my father said simply, "No matter how many times you are betrayed, it is always better to forgive than to live in a spirit of anger and mistrust." I was deeply impressed by his attitude, but I was also horrified. How would I react, I wondered, if I were treated in such a way?

In 1980 I found out. My church suddenly asked me to step down from my work as assistant elder to my father, a task I had been appointed to almost ten years earlier. To this day I am not completely sure why it happened. Most probably there was an element of the same divisive jealousy that had resulted in my father's expulsion forty years earlier. Whatever the reason, the very same people who had always praised and encouraged me – including several friends, colleagues, and even several close relatives – began to find fault with everything I had ever done.

Confused and angry, I was tempted to fight back. My father was by then senior elder of four large congregations, and he needed me more than ever; only weeks before, my mother had died of cancer. On top of that, I couldn't see what I had done wrong. True, I was known to be blunt about what I felt, especially in matters where I felt that politeness or diplomacy would mask a real issue, and not everyone in our church appreciated this. Still, I had always tried to be humble and considerate. And now this! I desperately wanted to set my record straight and re-establish my "rightful" place.

Papa, however, refused to support me in fighting back. Instead he pointed me to the Sermon on the Mount, where Jesus speaks of forgiving others for their trespasses so that we, too, may be forgiven. He reminded me that in the end we won't have to answer for what others do to us – only for what we do to them.

Suddenly I realised I wasn't as blameless as I had thought I was. I began to see that deep down I held grudges against various members of my church, and that instead of trying to justify myself, I needed to get down on my knees and ask God to forgive me. Then I would find strength to forgive.

I did this, and right away it seemed as if a dam had burst open somewhere deep down inside my heart. Before, my struggle had centred on the pain of hurt pride; now I was able to see things from a new perspective – and it all seemed rather petty.

With a new determination to set things straight and take the blame for whatever tensions existed, I went to everyone I felt I might have hurt in some way in the past, and asked them to forgive me. As I went from one person to the next, the knots in my heart seemed to undo themselves one by one, and by the end of it I felt like a new person.

That year was a very painful one for me, but it was also an important one, because it taught me several lessons I will never forget. First, it does not matter if people misunderstand you or accuse you unjustly. What matters is standing right before God. Second, even though the decision to forgive must always come from within, it is never a matter of willpower alone. The most powerful source of strength is always your own need – your own acknowledgment of weakness and your own experience of being forgiven. Finally, if your forgiveness is going to bear fruit, the soil around it – the soil of the heart – must be soft enough for it to grow in. If it is not soft – if you are not willing to be humble and vulnerable – your forgiveness will never be more than a fruitless gesture.

Humility and vulnerability are not easy virtues to acquire. In my experience, they come only with hard work, practice, patience, and pain. Still, life is poorer without them. As M. Scott Peck writes:

> There is no way that we can live a rich life unless we are willing to suffer repeatedly, experiencing depression and despair, fear and anxiety, grief and sadness, anger and the agony of forgiving, confusion and doubt, criticism and rejection. A life lacking these emotional upheavals will not only be useless to ourselves; it will be useless to others. We cannot heal without being willing to be hurt.

Forgiveness and Marriage

People ask me what advice I have for a married couple
struggling in their relationship. I always answer: pray and
forgive. And to young people from violent homes, I say:
pray and forgive. And again, even to the single mother
with no family support: pray and forgive.

MOTHER TERESA

Over many years of marriage counselling, I have seen
again and again that unless a husband and wife forgive each
other daily, marriage can become a living hell. I have also
seen that the thorniest problems can often be resolved with
three simple words: I am sorry.

Asking one's partner for forgiveness is always difficult,
because it requires humility, vulnerability, and the acknowledgment of weakness and failure. Yet there are few things
that make a marriage more healthy.

Dietrich Bonhoeffer, the German pastor imprisoned by
Hitler for his opposition to the Nazi regime, used to tell

the members of the small community he founded about the need to "live together in forgiveness," because without forgiveness no human fellowship – least of all a marriage – can survive. "Don't insist on your rights," he once wrote. "Don't blame each other, don't judge or condemn each other, don't find fault with each other, but accept each other as you are, and forgive each other every day from the bottom of your hearts."

In forty-three years of marriage, my wife, Verena, and I have had no lack of opportunities to test our willingness to forgive. Only a week after our wedding we had our first crisis. We had invited my parents and sisters over to dinner in our new apartment, and Verena had spent all afternoon cooking. My sister, an artist, had made us a set of pottery dishes, and I set the table with them.

My family arrived and we sat down to eat. Suddenly both ends of the table collapsed – I had not snapped the hinged extensions properly into place. Food and broken pottery covered the floor, and my wife fled the room in tears. It was hours before she could forgive me and laugh about the disaster, which has since become a family legend.

By the time we had eight children, there were plenty of opportunities for disagreements. Every evening Verena would bath the children and get them into their pyjamas, after which she would have them wait for me on the couch with their favourite picture books. As soon as I came home

The author and his wife on their wedding day

from work, however, they all wanted to go outdoors again
and play with me, so we often ended up romping in the
garden. Afterwards, Verena had to clean up the children
all over again, which she did, though not without a little
justified grumbling.

Most of our children suffered from asthma, and when
they were small they woke us almost nightly with their
coughing and wheezing. This, too, became a source of occa-
sional tensions, especially when Verena reminded me that I
could get out of bed and help them just as well as she could.

There were arguments over my work as well. As a sales-
man for our publishing house, I spent countless days on the

road. And because my territory covered western New York State – Buffalo, Rochester and Syracuse – I was often a good six or eight hours' drive away from home. Later my work took me to Canada, Europe, Africa, and even Australia. I always ended up defending such trips as vitally important, but this did little to soothe Verena, who packed my suitcases and stayed behind with the children.

Then there was *The New York Times*. After a hard day on the road, I couldn't see the harm in stretching out with the paper for a few minutes while the children played around me, and I told my wife so. Only later did I realise that it would have been nice to acknowledge the fact that she, too, had been working all day. At the time, I tended to bristle when she reminded me.

I often think about how our marriage might have turned out if we hadn't learned to forgive each other on a daily basis right from the start. So many couples sleep in the same bed and share the same house but remain miles apart inwardly, because they have built up a wall of resentment between themselves. The bricks in this wall may be very small – a forgotten anniversary, a misunderstanding, a business meeting that took precedence over a long-awaited family outing.

Many marriages could be saved by the simple realisation that a spouse will never be perfect. Too often, couples assume that a healthy relationship is one that is free from disagreements. Unable to live up to such an unrealistic expectation, they either bottle up their true feelings about each other, or else give up, disillusioned, and separate on grounds of "incompatibility."

Human imperfection means that we will make mistakes and hurt each other, unknowingly and even knowingly. In my own personal life I have found that the only fail-safe solution is to forgive, seventy times seven if necessary. C. S. Lewis writes:

> To forgive the incessant provocations of daily life – to keep on forgiving the bossy mother-in-law, the bullying husband, the nagging wife, the selfish daughter, the deceitful son – how can we do it? Only, I think, by remembering where we stand, by meaning our words when we say in our prayers each night, "Forgive our trespasses as we forgive those who trespass against us."

The power of forgiveness is wonderfully illustrated by the story of my wife's parents, Hans and Margrit Meier. Hans was a strong-willed man, and his stubbornness caused more than one period of separation in their marriage.

An ardent anti-militarist, Hans was imprisoned only months after their wedding in 1929 because he refused to join the Swiss army. Shortly after his release, the couple was separated again. She had discovered the faith community my grandparents founded and wanted to join it, whereas he

Hans and Margrit Meier

was not interested. Having recently given birth to their first child, Margrit begged Hans to join them, but he would not be easily swayed. It was several months before she convinced him to come.

Thirty years and eleven children later, they separated a third time, again over differences regarding their commitment to their church. Hans moved to Buenos Aires, where he remained for the next eleven years. Margrit and most of their children, including Verena, emigrated to the United States.

There were no signs of outward rancour, but there were no signs of healing either. Slowly, a wall of bitterness rose up which threatened to keep them apart forever. When Verena and I married in 1966, Hans did not even attend the wedding.

In 1972 I went to Buenos Aires with Verena's brother, Andreas, in an attempt to forge some kind of reconciliation with Hans, but he wasn't interested – at least not at first. He only wanted to recount his side of the story and let us know, once again, how many times he had been hurt. On the last day of our trip, though, something changed. He announced that he would visit us in the United States. He insisted that he would come for just two weeks, and emphasised the fact that he had a return ticket, but it was a start.

When the visit finally materialised, we were disappointed. Hans simply could not forgive. We made every effort to clear up past misunderstandings and acknowledged our guilt in the events leading up to his long estrangement, but we weren't getting anywhere. Intellectually, Hans knew that the only thing standing between us was his inability to forgive. Yet he could not bring himself to do it.

Then came the turning point. In the middle of a discussion that was going nowhere, my uncle Hans-Hermann, who was dying of lung cancer, summoned all his strength, stood up, came over to Hans, and tapped him on the chest saying, "Hans, the change must happen here!" These words cost a tremendous effort: my uncle was receiving supplemental oxygen through nasal tubes and was barely able to speak at the time.

Hans was completely disarmed. His coldness melted away, and he decided then and there to forgive – and to return to his wife and family. After travelling back to Argentina to wind up his affairs, he moved back in with them for good.

Thankfully, in all their years of separation, Hans and Margrit's bond was never completely broken: Hans never touched another woman, and Margrit prayed daily for her husband's return. Still, it took time for them to rebuild their relationship, and the key was surely their willingness to forgive. In the end, their marriage was fully restored to one of deep love and joy in each other. It lasted till Margrit's death sixteen years later.

The story of my parents-in-law shows that a marriage disrupted by long separation can be healed. But what about one broken by adultery? Is it ever fair to expect a cheated wife or husband to dredge up enough courage to forgive and start over again?

Three years ago I counselled Ed and Carol, a couple whose marriage was in shambles. Even before they were married, Ed had been a problem drinker, and this caused tensions in the house from the very start. Aside from that, however, things went fairly well, and they soon had children: first a boy, and then a girl. To any outsider, it would have seemed the perfect marriage. Inwardly, however, Ed and Carol were drifting further and further apart. Then Ed became involved with a neighbour and began an affair with her.

Ed and Carol joined our church a few years later, and around that time he confessed the affair, first to his wife and then to me. As he admitted later, his conscience gave him no peace, and he couldn't stand the pressure of keeping such a secret while pretending that everything was fine.

Carol was dumbfounded. She had sensed for a long time that something was wrong, but she had never imagined such deception. Seething, she told Ed that their marriage was over, and that she would never forgive him.

Though it wasn't hard to sympathise with Carol's anger, I felt that her initial reaction – "I'll never forgive you" – had less to do with the difficulty of forgiving Ed than with the idea of fairness or justice or "getting back" at him. I am sure that deep down she still wanted nothing more than a healthy relationship with the man she loved – the father of her children. But because of the way he had trampled on her, first with his drinking, and then with his adultery, she could not let go of her indignation. Ed didn't deserve another chance, and right now she wasn't going to give him one...

If anything was clear to me, it was that both Ed and Carol needed time and space to work through their problems on their own. For one thing, they were in no state to stay together, and there could be no quick fix. A new relationship had to be built from the bottom up, and the process would be long and painful. For another, I felt that a temporary separation would give them the objectivity they needed to see each other with new eyes, and might even help them rediscover their original love for each other.

Ed and Carol separated, and for the next months I counselled each of them separately. Ed needed help to see the gravity of his unfaithfulness, which he convinced me he wanted to do, while Carol needed help to see that until she forgave him, the deep wounds he had inflicted on her would never heal. As she herself recognised, her worst fear after learning of Ed's affair had been that he would leave her for good, and she didn't want that to happen, so she would have to make it clear to him that she was willing to take him back.

Later, at Carol's request, they began to communicate by phone calls. Then, as their conversations grew longer and more relaxed, they decided they were ready to try meeting face to face again. Carol still had her ups and downs, but as time went on she found herself wanting to give life with Ed another try – and not just for the sake of the children, who had stayed with her when he had moved out of the house, but for her own sake as well. More important, she admitted that Ed's unfaithfulness had not been solely his fault, and that she too bore a guilt for their estrangement. Meanwhile Ed had stopped drinking and begun to assure Carol in other ways as well that he was going to make their marriage work.

Finally, after ten months, Ed and Carol moved back together. In a special service held to celebrate their new beginning, they publicly forgave each other and re-consecrated their marriage. Then, faces beaming, they exchanged new rings.

In a society like ours, where one out of every two marriages ends in divorce, it is tempting to condemn couples who do not stay together. Naturally no one has a right to do that. But after seeing the healing effects of forgiveness in dozens of marriages, including foundering ones like Ed and Carol's, I find it impossible to suppress the hope that hundreds of thousands more could be saved.

Forgiving a Parent

It is freeing to become aware that we do not have to be victims of our past and can learn new ways of responding. But there is a step beyond this recognition…It is the step of forgiveness. Forgiveness is love practiced among people who love poorly. It sets us free without wanting anything in return.

HENRI J. M. NOUWEN

In a world where countless people have been scarred by childhood abuse – psychological, physical, or sexual – it is no wonder that television and radio programmes, newspapers and magazines never tire of the theme, but follow one lurid story after another, day after day. On talk show after talk show, survivors pour out their anguish to a curious but ultimately jaded and uncaring public. Yet no amount of soul-baring seems to bring them the healing they seek. How and where can they find it?

Obviously, the dynamics of every family, as well as the particulars of each instance of abuse, make it useless to offer generic advice or suggestions. Still, the following stories show that the possibility of reconciling should never be ruled out, even in the case of the cruellest parent. They also show the resilience of the human spirit, even when it has been beaten down, and the hope that springs from the mysterious source of strength we call love, whenever we are willing to draw from it.

Don grew up on an Appalachian farm in an extended family of some forty relatives. All of them shared one house and eked out a living on the same small plot of land. His childhood was brutal: he tells of cousins who tried to hang one another and a grandmother who fired at disobedient children with a shotgun full of rock salt.

When Don was about ten his father found a new job and took his wife and children to Long Island. Once there the family's financial situation improved. But their relationships did not. Soon after the move, Don's mother abandoned her husband and children, who were left at the mercy of their father. He beat them so routinely that they lived in constant fear of him. Don still remembers the sick feeling that returned to his stomach each afternoon as he got off the school bus and thought about what the evening might bring.

Then one day Don's father was seriously injured in a collision that left him paralysed from the neck down. Once the tyrant of the household, he was now a quadriplegic, utterly dependent on others to care for his daily needs.

Most people from such a home would escape as soon as possible, but not Don. With every reason in the world to abandon his father, he remained at his side for years, feeding him and washing, dressing, and exercising the lifeless limbs that had once beat him mercilessly, sometimes to the point of unconsciousness. (Now married, Don has arranged for a hired nurse to provide his father with 24-hour care, but he still lives nearby and visits him frequently.)

Pressed for an explanation, Don has little to say. He never saw his decision to stay on at home as a heroic or sacrificial deed. He never really even thought about it. But what was the option? How could he leave home, when the man who had brought him into the world – his own father – was as helpless as a baby and there was no one to care for him? "Dad needed me, so I stayed."

Bad memories of the past still haunt Don on occasion, and he says his father still has his demons to fight. Life isn't all roses, by any means. But at least they can talk and share the burdens of the emotional battles they have to wage. And in caring for his father Don says he has finally found a measure of the happiness he yearned for as a child. "Call it forgiveness if you like," he says. Whatever it is, it has brought him wholeness and a sense of healing.

Karl Keiderling, a family friend who died several years ago in his eighties, suffered a similarly harsh childhood. The only son of a German working-class family, his early years were clouded by the First World War and the economic devastation that followed it. His mother died when he was four, and his stepmother when he was fourteen. To make matters worse, his father saw him as a burden on the family. When, after his stepmother's death, his father put out an ad in the hopes of finding a new mother for his children, he intentionally excluded Karl: "Widower with three daughters looking for a housekeeper; possibility of future marriage."

Several women applied, and in the end one decided to stay. It was only afterwards that she found out about the existence of a boy in the house, which she never quite got over. Karl's food was always poorer than the rest of the family's, and she complained about him day in and day out.

Karl's father, for his part, was silent in the face of his new wife's tirades, and did nothing to defend his son. In fact, he joined her in mistreating the boy and often beat him. His instrument of choice was a leather strap mounted with brass rings. Karl tried to protect himself on occasion, but that only infuriated his father and earned him extra blows to his head and face.

Unlike Don, Karl left home as soon as he could. Attracted by the youth movement sweeping Europe in those years,

he joined ranks with a group of young blue-collar social-
ists who were set on changing the world. Eventually his
wanderings brought him to the rural commune where my
grandparents lived. There, my grandfather welcomed him
with an embrace and said, "We've been waiting for you
to arrive."

Karl immediately felt at home and decided to stay. He
threw himself vigorously into the work, chopping wood,
hauling water, and tending the garden. But the agony
of his childhood, as well as his feelings of resentment
toward his father and stepmother, didn't leave him. Day
after day his bitterness grew, hanging around him like
a heavy cloud and threatening to block out everything
good.

Finally Karl went to my grandfather and poured out his
need. The response he got astounded him: "Write to your
parents and ask their forgiveness for every instance in which
you might have hurt their feelings or otherwise caused them
grief. And look only at your own guilt, not theirs." Karl was
taken aback, so much so that it took him some time before
he felt ready to write. But eventually he did, and amazingly,
his father answered the letter.

He never apologised for the way he had beaten Karl as
a boy, or acknowledged any guilt of his own. But Karl said
it no longer mattered. Through forgiving, he himself had
found freedom from the anger that had weighed on him,

and a deep sense of peace. Karl never complained about his childhood again.

Maria, a relative from my wife's side of the family, overcame her resentment toward her abusive father in a similar way:

> My mother died at the age of forty-two, leaving behind my father and eight children, aged one to nineteen. Mother's death was devastating for the whole family, but especially for my father, and he suffered an emotional breakdown just when we needed him most. One of the results of his instability was a lack of self-control, and he tried to molest my sister and me. I began to avoid him, and then to hate him.
>
> Soon after this my father moved away, and I left South America for school in Germany. I didn't see him for another seven years. But I held on to my hatred, and it grew inside me.
>
> Later I returned from Europe and became engaged to a childhood friend. My father asked me if we could meet. I flatly refused. I had no desire to see him.
>
> When my fiancé found out about it, however, he did not understand how I could refuse such a meeting. If my father had expressed a longing for reconciliation, wasn't it my duty to respond? It cost me quite a battle to come around to my fiancé's point of view, but he was insistent, and in the end I agreed.

We met my father in a café, found a table, and sat down. Before I had a chance to say a word, he turned to me, broken, and asked for my forgiveness. Disarmed, I melted and assured him of my forgiveness on the spot. There was no way I could have withheld it.

Despite the apparent ease with which Don and Maria forgave their fathers, child abuse is probably the most difficult thing in the world to recover from. Given the imbalance of power between the adult (the perpetrator) and the child (the victim), the blame is always one-sided. And why should the innocent forgive the guilty?

Tragically, many victims of child abuse mistakenly believe that they share some of the blame. They worry that somehow they must have brought on or even deserved what was done to them. In fact, much of the power an abuser holds over his victim, even after the physical abuse itself has stopped, comes from this misguided notion of complicity. It is part of the victimisation.

To make matters worse, some people claim that when a victim forgives an abuser, he is implying that he – the victim – is at least partly to blame. Nothing, of course, could be further from the truth. Forgiveness is necessary simply because both victim and victimiser – who in most cases know one another (or are even related) – are prisoners of a shared darkness in which both will remain bound until someone opens the door. Forgiveness is the only way out, and even if an abuser chooses to remain in the darkness, that should not hold the victim back.

Kate, a neighbour in her fifties, was abused by her alcoholic mother for years but is now reconciled to her. Like others, her journey shows that when a victim is changed by the willingness to forgive, her abuser may be affected and transformed as well.

> I was born in a small Canadian town shortly after World War II, the eldest of five children. Father's construction job was twenty-five miles away, and between travel and a twelve-hour workday he spent very little time at home.
>
> Money was always a problem, and there were other tensions in our family, though I couldn't explain them. All I knew was that the older I got, the more things seemed to go downhill, especially after the birth of my youngest brother, when I was nine. In retrospect it's very clear what happened: Mother had started drinking.

After Kate's mother began to come home drunk, her parents separated. There was no family life to speak of; the house was neglected, and the laundry was never washed. Everything depended on thirteen-year-old Kate.

> By the time Jamie, the youngest, started school, Mother was almost never at home. I never managed to do any

homework and was not learning very much. I completely failed ninth grade and had to repeat it the following year.

Later two of my sisters left home, found jobs, and rented an apartment in town. But I stayed. Somebody had to look after the little ones. And as poorly as I did it, at least they were given something to eat.

Then Mother found out about a new source of additional income: in an effort to relieve overcrowding at the local hospital for the mentally and physically disabled, the government was paying people to put up "surplus" patients in their own homes. Mother took in two older men and a woman.

I had to give up my bed to one of the men and share a double bed with the woman, who rarely slept. When I told Mother that I couldn't cope with this and wanted the hospital to take the woman back, she wouldn't hear of it. After all, there was a cheque coming in every month.

Mother said she'd come home in the evenings to help me, and for a while she did. But the drunken state she came home in! Then she'd say that if it wasn't for me, she wouldn't be in such a mess. At first I didn't understand what she meant, but later I found out: my parents had been forced to marry because my mother was already carrying me.

At times Mother became physically abusive. Then in the morning, if she asked me about the bruises on my face and I told her that she had done it, she claimed I was lying.

At sixteen, Kate quit school in order to devote herself totally to the care of her siblings. Around that time she met her husband, Tom, whom she married two years later. She still remembers the guilt she felt when her mother asked accusingly, "Who is going to do the work around here?" Nonetheless, she moved out of the house, and soon she and Tom were raising a family of their own.

> At this point I just wanted to forget about my mother. I had my own little family, and I had Tom's parents, who loved my children. Then, suddenly my mother wanted to re-establish contact. I refused. I finally had some leverage, and I was going to pay her back.
>
> By this time my parents' divorce was finalized, and Mother had stopped drinking. Remarkably enough she had come to realise that the combination of alcohol and the blood-pressure medications she was taking would kill her. All the same, I had no desire to visit her. I simply could not trust her.

A few years later, after the birth of another child, Kate found out that her husband had taken a call from her mother, who had asked if she could visit the family. Tom had told her she was welcome.

> I was hopping mad. I told Tom, "You call her right back and tell her she can't come. Tell her whatever you want to tell her. This is my baby, and I'm not willing to share it with her." I was very nasty. Later, however, I began to feel bad, and I went to talk to our pastor. I thought maybe he would have a solution.

As I explained my dilemma to him, he sat there and listened to me. I finished, but he didn't say anything. I waited. I felt fully justified in having done what I did, but I wanted his assurance. I didn't get it. All he said was, "You have to come to peace with your mother."

I said, "You don't know my mother."

He replied, "That has nothing to do with it."

Meanwhile my mother came anyway. She was not well when she arrived, and she needed a lot of care. I did not make it easy for her.

Then, during the last few days of her visit, I sensed that there was something she was trying to tell me. She even seemed willing to listen to what I had to say to her. As we talked, I realised that Mother wanted a new relationship (by then I desperately wanted one, too) and that she was determined to remove whatever was in the way. It was then that I knew I had to forgive her, so I did. Immediately a wave of relief and healing came over me. It was indescribable, and it has stayed with me to this day.

Not all instances of parent-child estrangement are so black and white. Susan, a Californian from very different circumstances, never suffered real abuse at the hands of her parents. Still she was embittered for years by her mother's personality, which she felt to be distant and cold. And like Kate, she found that the only route to mutual healing was to face her own lack of love and declare a willingness to forgive.

Ever since I can remember, I have had a difficult relationship with my mother. I feared her angry outbursts, her biting, sarcastic tongue, and I never felt able to please her. As a consequence, I began to nurse a deep anger toward her – a smouldering, hidden anger that made me close myself off to her. I nursed memories of injustices from early childhood, of sharp words and a few blows (none worth remembering). I became extremely sensitive to her reproofs and easily felt rejected.

Somehow we just never had an open, trusting relationship. Instead I looked to the other adults in my life, especially my teachers. My mother resented my attachment to them but was never able to express it. I can remember wishing to be taken out of my family, to be adopted by one of them. I can also remember a strong physical feeling of not belonging that would come over me in waves. But in my desire to be accepted, I tried to be "good" and hid my true feelings.

Things only became worse as I grew into adolescence. I found more and more ways to subtly act out my anger and do what I wanted to do. I also found more ways to sneak around my mother. I even "got back" at her by having a secret affair with our parish priest, who often socialised with my parents.

That relationship eventually ended, and I went off to college and a place of my own. Then I married. Still, I continued to be at odds with my mother. It was actually a very strange relationship, because I still desperately wanted to please her.

Mom went through extended periods of physical and emotional crisis over those years, but I found it difficult to sympathise or even show much interest. I finally reached out to her when she was going through a twelve-step programme for alcoholics. We had a wonderful week of talking and sharing, but then suddenly the doors closed again. I blamed it on her, though I cannot now say why.

Finally it became clear to me that her strong, self-confident, in-control exterior was just a shell for a very insecure person underneath, and that she was nursing plenty of hurts from her own childhood. We were both trying to reach out to one another in our own way, but both of us were so afraid of rejection that we couldn't be honest with each other. Our efforts were superficial at best.

The breakthrough came a few years later when I was hounded by a friend to listen to a tape of a talk by some writer called Charles Stanley. I had never heard of him, but I was looking for answers to several big questions at the time, so I listened – guardedly. I can't remember exactly what he said, but it was something about relationships, and it was just what I needed to hear at the time. It helped me to see that insofar as my mother and I were estranged, we each had a share of guilt, and until one of us asked the other for forgiveness, the rift might never be breached.

Not long after that I visited my parents. When I was alone with my mother, I asked her to forgive me for the way I had treated her in the past and told her I forgave her too. I admitted that I had been angry at her all of my life, even though I wasn't sure why. She didn't understand why

I should be angry, but she too apologised for the hurt she had caused. She said, "What has happened has happened, and we can't change that. But we can move on."

For anyone who feels trapped in the quagmire of a difficult relationship, these words are as vital as they are simple. No one can undo the past. But each of us can choose to forgive, and each of us can move on.

Blaming God

It is not right to try to remove all suffering, nor is it right to endure it stoically. Suffering can be used, turned to good account. What makes a life happy or unhappy is not outward circumstances, but our inner attitude to them.

EBERHARD ARNOLD

In most cases, when the subject of forgiving comes up, we think of it in terms of our willingness (or unwillingness) to stop blaming a person who has hurt us. Sometimes, though, an injury has no human cause, and try as we might, we cannot find anyone who is truly at fault.

To those who have no belief in God, the result may be a sense of undirected annoyance at the hand dealt them by life. To those who believe, the result is often anger at God. Frustrated by our inability to pin down a reason for our pain, which we are quick to see as unjustified and undeserved, we rebel against it and accuse God. "How can a merciful God permit *this?*" In the end, our frustration may turn to resentment, or even to rage.

In many ways, it is easier (even for someone who doesn't actually believe in a higher power) to blame God than to face the possibility that there really might be no one to blame. Anger is a legitimate stage of grief, even when there's no obvious target for us to direct it at. It needs to be expressed and dealt with if we hope to find healing and move on.

Still, it is fruitless to stay angry at God. We can hold him responsible for hurting us, but he cannot very well apologise. If there is anything to be done about circumstances we wish we could change, but can't, it is to accept them gracefully. In doing so we may find that even the greatest obstacle can become an opportunity for growth.

Whenever I am tempted to blame God, I remember a period of great frustration I went through several years ago, and what I learned from it. It all began on the way home from a fishing trip in upstate New York – a welcome chance to escape the pressures of my work for a few days – when I noticed that I was losing my voice. At first I ignored it, expecting it to improve within several days. But it only grew worse. Finally my doctor referred me to a specialist. The diagnosis: a paralysed vocal chord.

The specialist reassured me that my voice would eventually recover, but weeks and then months went by, and there was no change. His prescription was complete voice rest (I wasn't even allowed to whisper) and frustrating as it was, I held to it religiously. Still there was no improvement. I wondered if I would ever speak again.

To make things worse, right during this time my congregation became embroiled in an extended crisis involving a fallout between several longstanding members. At meeting after meeting I was asked for my input as senior pastor, but instead of being able to respond, I could only sit by in silence and write down the things I most wanted to say.

When a capability like speech – or anything else we take for granted – is taken away from us, we can choose to see it with new appreciation, as the gift it is. But I was too anxious and upset to do that. To be honest, I was angry. Even if God was testing me, I said to myself, he couldn't have picked a worse time.

It was only with time that I was able to see the whole annoying predicament from another angle: I began to realise that it was providing me with an important chance to develop a more flexible outlook on life, to take myself less seriously, and to make the best of an imperfect situation. Three months later, my voice began to return; now, seven years later, it is back to normal. But I have never forgotten those twelve weeks.

Andrea, a woman in my church, struggled to accept a much heavier burden: she miscarried three times before having a healthy child. Unlike mine, Andrea's story is not, strictly speaking, about blaming or "forgiving" God. For her the battle was to accept the loss of her babies without succumbing to the fear that God was somehow trying to punish her. But in showing how she was able to wrestle through her emotions and find peace, it illustrates a similar theme.

Neil and I were delighted to find that I was pregnant after only six months of marriage. But one night, just before Christmas, I felt intense pain that grew rapidly worse. Our doctor wanted to send me to the hospital, and our neighbour, a nurse, came to stay with me until we left for town. She confirmed my worst fears – I would probably lose my baby. The emotional pain was at least as severe as the physical. Why, God? Why me? Why do you have to take away this tiny soul so soon? What have I done wrong?

In order to save my life, an operation was necessary. The baby was lost, and I spent weeks recuperating. What a different Christmas this had become!

We agonised over our loss and felt alone in our pain. When one of our relatives said to us, "Cheer up! Maybe you'll have better luck next time," I felt like I had been slapped in the face. Luck? We had just lost a baby, a real person, a child!

Someone sent me a card that said, "The Lord giveth, and the Lord taketh away, blessed be the name of the

Lord." That made me really upset. How could I thank God for this horrible, painful experience? I couldn't. And I couldn't stop thinking that somehow God was punishing me, even though I couldn't understand why.

Our pastor consoled me: God is a God of love, not of punishment, and he is there to ease our pain. I grasped at his words as a drowning person grabs onto a pole held out from the shore. Neil's loving support seemed like a visible sign of this love, and we discovered that our pain united us in a new way. The words "Weeping shall endure for the night, but joy comes in the morning" especially comforted me, even when I couldn't feel that joy coming, when it seemed that dawn would never break.

Slowly, with time and with the loving help of those around me, I was able to feel that this deeply painful experience had given me an inkling of the love of God, who cares about the suffering of people and who was, I am convinced, right there beside me in my pain. God became more real to me, and I began to trust his love.

But then, some months later, when I was expecting another baby and hoping fervently that all would go well, the same thing happened again. Severe pain, an emergency trip to the hospital, and an operation to save my life. Again another precious little person lost just after it had come into being. Deep pain tore my heart apart. I wrote in my diary: "I cannot see why; perhaps I never will. I need the assurance of faith – Help me!"

Neil stood faithfully beside me. He had lost a sister to cancer some years before, and what he had written then was a great source of sustenance: "We are separated from God only in physical distance, and that distance is perhaps not great." I hung on to that with all my strength.

Slowly, over weeks and months, the pain of loss lessened, although it has never departed entirely. About a year later I again lost an unborn child. Once more there was deep pain in my heart, but this time no desperation over why.

Today Andrea is the mother of a beautiful six-year-old daughter. Although thinking about her first three pregnancies always brings back a flood of emotions, she is not bitter. In fact, she is even able to point to two good fruits of her anguish: a greater love for her husband, who "went to hell and back with me," and endless gratitude for her only child.

Like Andrea, Jon and Gretchen Rhoads – a young couple in a nearby town – eagerly awaited the birth of their first child. Alan was born after a seemingly normal pregnancy, and in the beginning everything seemed all right. After he was discharged from the hospital, though, his parents noticed something was wrong. Very wrong. Alan didn't eat well. His muscle tone was poor. He lay very still, almost without moving, and when he breathed, he occasionally made strange gurgling sounds.

Alan was quickly admitted to a nearby university hospital, but he was three months old before his problems became clear: he would never walk or talk; he was blind; and he had significant abnormalities of the hips, brain, ears, and stomach.

Jon and Gretchen were devastated. They had long suspected that something was wrong, but they hadn't expected it to be this bad. Right away they began to accuse themselves, and it wasn't long before they began to accuse God: Why us?

Jon says that though he was angry, he could never really say at whom. Himself? Gretchen? Alan's doctors? God? Yes, perhaps God, but he couldn't explain why. Still, he refused to become bitter, but concluded instead that "either God does not love us, or this is just how Alan is meant to be. We may never know why, but if we are resentful about Alan's condition, we will kill any joy we have had in him."

Both Jon and Gretchen admit that acceptance is easier to talk about, than to actually practise. There have been plenty of times when they wanted to run away from it all, when they simply couldn't face another visitor offering meaningless words of sympathy.

And while some days bring progress and new hope, others bring setbacks and trials. In his first year alone Alan had a tracheotomy and numerous other surgeries, including an appendectomy. How much more suffering will he have to endure?

In a world quick to offer "early diagnosis" and abortion as the answer to imperfect babies, Alan's parents refuse to see their child as a burden. "He has a great deal to tell us," Gretchen wrote when he was almost one, "and we are not about to let him go."

His small hand reaches up through a tangle of wires to find my cheek. As I stoop to lift him from his bed, his eyelids lift slightly and he gives me a sleepy grin...In the eleven months since his birth, Alan has been hospitalised five times; we have long since stopped counting the outpatient appointments. Each time we come home with more questions and fewer answers; more tears, and less certainty. But as he snuggles against me and looks around curiously, he grins. His smile is a balm to my heart.

How much more pain can Alan bear? What new hurdles await us? His tracheostomy has taken away the few small adventures we had looked forward to: bottles and the chance to explore solid food. No more gurgles of joy, either, and no more cries of frustration.

If he lives, the doctor tells us, he may outgrow the need for these tubes. If he lives. The words cut me to my heart, and yet his smile continues to give me hope. He is teaching me acceptance every day.

In the end, it is this acceptance Gretchen writes of that allows us to "forgive" God. Without it, we are left rebelling against our lot in life, and fighting every cross we feel unjustly forced to bear. With it, we gain the ability to see our hardships in relation to the suffering of others, and strength to carry them.

Today, despite the predictions of the doctors who examined him as a baby, Alan is a sunny, outgoing teen. He can walk and run – and even dance. Visit his home, and he may pedal out to meet you on his tricycle. Though he can't verbalise (and is still dependent on a feeding tube) he has no problem communicating, be it with a handshake, a wave, a grunt, or a mischievous laugh.

"At the beginning," his father says, "we saw Alan first and foremost in terms of his disabilities. We prayed for him to be healed, and for his handicaps to be overcome. As the years passed, we grew wiser. Now we pray that *we* may be healed, and that we might find the qualities that make him so perfect – perfect in his innocence and love, in tears and laughter."

In his mother's words, "Of course, it's not all roses with Alan, and when there are decisions to be made, we worry over whether we are doing the right thing. There are also our other children: I fret about whether we give enough time and attention to them. But in grappling with these questions, we constantly come back to forgiveness. Our parenting depends on it. Our marriage depends on it. To

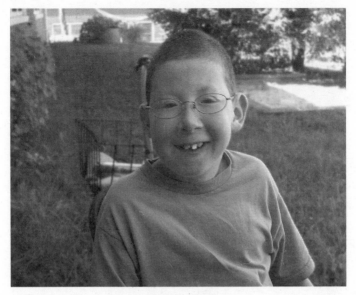

Alan Rhoads

be able to say 'I'm sorry' to each other, to our children, and to God is so vital. That's what lets us start over afresh, with our hearts at peace – ready to laugh with Alan as he cranks up the volume on his favourite music and tugs at our hands to get us to dance with him."

Forgiving Ourselves

Without being forgiven, released from the consequences of what we have done, our capacity to act would, as it were, be confined to a single deed from which we could never recover; we would remain the victims of its consequences forever, not unlike the sorcerer's apprentice who lacked the magic formula to break the spell.

HANNAH ARENDT

When we assure a person who has hurt us that we no longer hold anything against him, all he has to do is accept our kindness – at least that is what we might hope. But that is often more easily said than done. For many people, the problem of guilt cannot be solved with another's forgiveness, or by any external means at all. For them, peace of mind comes only when they are able to forgive themselves.

I first met Delf Fransham in 1953. That was the year he moved from the United States to the remote South American village where I grew up, and began to teach at the local school. There were eleven of us in his class, all boys, and all ruffians, and a few days into his first term we decided to put him to the test.

One typical Paraguayan morning (humid and around 110 degrees), we offered to take him on a hike. Officially, we wanted to show him the sights. Privately, we wanted to see what he was made of. After leading him at least ten kilometres through jungle, prairie, and swampland, we finally turned back. Shortly after we arrived home he collapsed with heat stroke.

Delf was in bed for days, but we hardly gave it a thought. We had achieved exactly what we wanted – proved him a sissy. But we were in for a small surprise. The day he came back to school he said, "Boys, let's try that hike again." We couldn't believe it! We covered the same route again and, sure enough, this time he did not succumb to the heat. Delf won our respect and our hearts that day, and we trusted him from then on. (There was something else to it, too: a talented athlete, he taught us football and loved to play with us.)

Decades later, and only by chance, I found out why Delf had poured so much love and energy into reaching his students. He had lost a child of his own.

Nicholas was born when the Franshams were still living in the United States, and one day as Delf was backing a pick-up load of firewood into their driveway, twenty-month-old

Delf and Katie Fransham with John, Nicholas and Anna

Nicholas, who was playing outdoors, ran to meet his father. Delf did not see him until it was too late, and ran over him.

Katie, Delf's wife, was busy inside the house when he carried in their little boy, limp in his arms. She remembers:

> I was beside myself – absolutely frantic – but Delf steadied me. We took Nicholas to our doctor, who was also the coroner, and explained what had happened...
>
> There was never any question about forgiving my husband, as I knew I was just as much to blame. Likewise he did not blame me, only himself. We stood in our sorrow together.

Delf, however, could not forgive himself, and the accident haunted him for years. From then on, he went out of his way to make time for children – time he could not spend with the son he had killed.

Looking back, I remember how his eyes often glistened with tears, and wonder what it was that made them come. Was it that he saw his son in us? Was he imagining the boy his toddler would never become? Whatever the reason, it seems that Delf's determination to show love to others was his way of making up for the anguish he had caused himself and his family by unintentionally taking a life. I am convinced that it saved him from brooding, and from nursing his feelings of guilt. Through loving others he was able to forgive himself and regain a sense of wholeness and peace.

David Harvey, now nearly seventy, joined the army at sixteen, just before the end of World War II. After spending most of the rest of the war years in training, he was transferred to Africa, then Germany, Italy, Hong Kong, China and the Mediterranean. At first he enjoyed his time in the army, especially the camaraderie he felt among fellow soldiers. But then something happened that changed his life forever.

> Part of my service time was spent in Kenya, predominantly carrying out police duties and hunting "terrorists." Much of the time was spent patrolling jungle areas. During one of these patrols I was involved in a terrible accident.

While lying in wait for a band of "terrorists," we ourselves were ambushed. There was a lot of shooting and a lot of confusion, and misunderstood orders. The patrol split into two halves. My half walked in a straight line along an animal path, while the second half cleared the bush on each side. Those in the bush overtook those on the path, and we consequently ended up firing at each other. Directly to my front, the bushes parted and I fired, shooting the patrol commander in the head. Abandoning our mission, we carried the wounded man for sixteen hours through the jungle on a makeshift bamboo stretcher to get him the medical help he so desperately required.

Eventually there was a court of inquiry and, in military terms, I was exonerated of all blame. But my conscience gave me no peace. Four years later, my term of service in the army ended and I returned to civilian life. At first I found this very difficult. In the army I had been given a number instead of a name, trained to comply with any order without question, and to believe that anything I was told to do was correct. This did not fit in with civilian life. But slowly things returned to normal, and I had time to reminisce over my service career. The thing that always came to the forefront was the shooting of my comrade. Where was he? How was he? Had he even survived?

After a number of years, I started to make my own inquiries as to the whereabouts and welfare of my colleague. But all the avenues I tried drew a blank. I met ex-colleagues, each of whom had a different story as to what had become of him. Then in 1996 my wife, Marion, found a book which mentioned this very incident. I telephoned the author, who admitted that he hadn't seen him recently, but had heard that he was living in London.

I realised that I had drawn another blank. Frustrated, I decided to enlist the services of a local newspaper. They published my story and photograph in a weekly edition of their paper. Within forty-eight hours I had received a call from the person I had been seeking for years.

It was a difficult experience. After a number of telephone conversations, we arranged to meet each other at my house. In due course, he came bringing presents...to the man who had shot him! Because of me, he was paralysed down one side and had difficulty walking and moving his arm. I asked him, "Can you ever forgive me?" He just hugged me. He had already forgiven me.

John Plummer lives the quiet life of a Methodist pastor in a sleepy Virginia town these days, but things weren't always so. A helicopter pilot during the Vietnam War, he helped organize a napalm raid on the village of Trang Bang in 1972 – a bombing immortalised by the prize-winning photograph of one of its victims, Phan Thi Kim Phuc.

For the next twenty-four years, John was haunted by the photograph – an image that for many people captured the essence of the war: a naked and burned nine-year-old running toward the camera, with plumes of black smoke billowing in the sky behind her.

Phan Thi Kim Phuc and John Plummer

For twenty-four years John's conscience tormented him. He badly wanted to find the girl to tell her that he was sorry – but he could not. Turning in on himself, he grew more and more depressed (the collapse of two marriages didn't help), and he began to drink.

Then, in an almost unbelievable coincidence, John met Kim during an event at the Vietnam War Memorial on Veterans Day, 1996. Kim had come to Washington, D.C., to lay a wreath for peace; John had come with a group of former pilots unable to come to terms with their shared past, but determined to stick together anyway.

In a speech to the crowd, Kim introduced herself as the girl in the famous photograph. She still suffered immensely from her burns, she said, but she was not bitter, and she wanted people to know that others had suffered even more than she had: "Behind that picture of me, thousands and thousands of people...died. They lost parts of their bodies. Their whole lives were destroyed, and nobody took their picture."

Kim went on to say that although she could not change the past, she had forgiven the men who had bombed her village, and that she felt a calling to promote peace by fostering goodwill between America and Vietnam. John, beside himself, pushed through the crowds and managed to catch her attention before she was whisked away by a police escort. He identified himself as a former pilot in Vietnam and said that he felt responsible for the bombing of her village twenty-four years before. He says:

> Kim saw my grief, my pain, my sorrow...She held out her arms to me and embraced me. All I could say was "I'm sorry; I'm sorry" – over and over again. And at the same time she was saying, "It's all right, I forgive you."

John says that it was vital for him to meet face to face with Kim, and to tell her that he had agonised for years over her injuries. Without having had the chance to get that off his chest, he is not sure he could have ever forgiven himself. As it turned out, of course, he got even more than he hoped for: Kim forgave him.

Reflecting on the way the incident changed his life, John maintains that forgiveness is "neither earned nor even deserved, but a gift." It is also a mystery. He still can't quite grasp how a short conversation could wipe away a twenty-four-year nightmare.

Pat, another Vietnam veteran, is a gentle, quiet man who loves children and horses. In the seven years since I first met him, however, I have become aware that he has a darker side – one that centres on his inability to forgive himself:

> Death is on my mind a lot. The deaths I have caused – and wanting my own death – are with me every day. I joke around a lot with the people I work with. I have to, to hide the pain and to keep my mind from thinking. I need to laugh. Laughing keeps the blues away.
>
> But I cannot love. Part of my soul is missing, and it seems I won't ever get it back. I don't know if I can ever forgive myself for all of my wrongs. I live day to day, but I am tired all the time – tired. Will it ever end? I don't see how. It's been with me over twenty-five years now.

People like Pat are often urged to receive formal counselling, to join a support group, or to attend group therapy meetings so as to compare notes with others who have had similar experiences. He has done all of this, and still not found peace. Perhaps, like John, he wishes he could meet the families of those he killed – an unlikely opportunity – or bring the victims themselves back to life so he could ask their forgiveness – an obviously impossible one. So what should he do?

A conversation Robert Coles once had with the psychoanalyst Anna Freud may hint at an answer. Discussing an elderly client with a long and troubled psychological history, Freud suddenly concluded:

> You know, before we say goodbye to this lady, we should wonder among ourselves not only what to think – we do that all the time! – but what in the world we would want for her. Oh, I don't mean psychotherapy; she's had lots of that. It would take more years, I suspect, of psychoanalysis than the good Lord has given her...No, she's had her fill of "us," even if she doesn't know it...This poor old lady doesn't need us at all...What she needs...is forgiveness. She needs to make peace with her soul, not talk about her mind. There must be a God, somewhere, to help her, to hear her, to heal her...and we certainly aren't the ones who will be of assistance to her in that regard!

Freud's point is a valid one, even for a person who claims to have no belief in God. At some level, all of us must come to terms with the parts of ourselves that we wish we could erase. All of us yearn for the freedom to live without guilt. At some level, every one of us longs for forgiveness.

Yet when all is said and done, we cannot acquire it. Sometimes the person we have wronged is unable or unwilling to forgive us. Sometimes we are unable or unwilling to forgive ourselves. Even the best psychoanalysis, the most earnest confession of guilt, may not be enough to assure us of lasting relief or healing.

But the power of forgiveness still exists, and as John Plummer found out, it can work wonders even when we are sure that we have neither earned nor deserved it. It comes to us as a gift, often when we feel least worthy of receiving it. Finally, like any gift, it can be accepted or rejected. What we do with it is up to us.

Accepting Responsibility

In the confession of concrete sins the old man dies a painful, shameful death before the eyes of a brother. Because this humiliation is so hard, we continually scheme to avoid it. Yet in the deep mental and physical pain of humiliation before a brother we experience our rescue and salvation.

DIETRICH BONHOEFFER

No one who has read this far will deny that forgiveness can bring about healing, even where healing seemed impossible. Its power might be mysterious, but it is clearly there, and it is so strong that people are sometimes swept away by it against their more rational instincts. All the same it is dangerous to become glib about forgiveness – to act as if it could be plucked off the nearest tree.

Certainly forgiveness is sometimes given and received lightly, or used to whitewash the ugly underside of life. But such forgiveness has no staying power. Even the most genuine declaration of forgiveness will wear thin if it is not accompanied by a change of heart, both in the forgiver and the forgiven. In other words, it must cost something if it is to have any lasting effect.

There is, moreover, little value in seeking forgiveness if we let it touch us only momentarily and then slide back into the same behaviour that required an apology in the first place. It is true that forgiveness is a gift and that it comes with no strings attached. But it is a useless one unless we let it change us for the better.

Mark and Debbie, friends of mine who used to be part of a small house church on the West Coast, experienced this hard reality firsthand:

> Over the years we witnessed the disastrous results of ignoring wrongdoing or secretly hiding it. We lived in a small urban community with several people, one of whom was a single man who had fallen in love with a married woman in our group. Some of us tried to tackle their affair by talking with them separately about it. Yet no one dared to bring it out in the open.
>
> Afraid of being judgemental, we chose to believe that this wasn't a very serious matter, at least not serious enough to bring it out into the open. Didn't we all make mistakes? Who were we to judge? We convinced ourselves that confrontation would not only add to their sense of shame and self-condemnation, but also perpetuate the cycle of failure. In the end we tried to forgive their shortcomings and avoided talking about them any further. Now we see that

this so-called compassion only perpetuated the problem... The man eventually left, and two years later, the woman he was involved with divorced her husband and followed him.

Far from being unique, incidents like this one are widespread. On the surface they may seem to have little to do with forgiveness, because there is never even a clear recognition of wrongdoing, and therefore no admission of the need for redemption. But at root they have everything to do with it. If, as in the case described above, the problem had been confronted, who knows how different the outcome might have been?

Obvious as it sounds, it is vital to remember that we cannot truly receive forgiveness until we acknowledge our need for it by admitting our wrongdoings to someone else, whether to the person we have hurt or (where that is not possible) to someone we trust. Some people dismiss this practice as "confession" – something for old-fashioned Catholics. Others admit that it can be helpful, but claim that guilt can be taken care of just as easily by recognising a misdeed and resolving not to repeat it. But that is utter foolishness: it is precisely such a recognition that brings about guilty feelings to begin with. That is why Tolstoy writes that the peace of heart attained by forgiving oneself in such a manner is nothing but "deadness of the soul." It is nothing like the real peace that comes to those who are humble and honest enough to ask those they have wronged for forgiveness.

Guilt works in secret, and it loses its power only when it is allowed out into the open. Often our desire to appear righteous keeps us from admitting our wrongs. Why reveal a foolish choice or a dumb mistake? Yet the more we try to push such things to the back of our minds, the more they will plague us, even if subconsciously. Eventually guilt will add to guilt, and we will become cramped and weighed down.

As for the freedom that comes from owning up to one's faults, Steve, an old friend of mine, says:

> In my search for inner peace I pursued various religions and studied psychology but never received more than partial answers. It was only after I saw my personal life for the shambles it was that I could see how urgently I needed to change, and how much I needed forgiveness.
>
> The pivotal experience came inexplicably and unexpectedly: I was suddenly aware what an enormous avalanche of wrongs I had left behind me. Before, this reality had been masked by pride and by my wanting to look good in front of others. But now, memories of everything I had ever done wrong poured out of me like a river of bile.
>
> All I wanted was to be free, to have nothing dark and ugly and hidden within me; I wanted to make good, wherever I could, the wrongs I had done. I had no excuses for

myself – youth, circumstances, or bad peers. I was responsible for what I had done.

On one page after another I poured it all out in clear detail. I felt as though an angel of repentance was slashing at my heart with his sword, such was the pain. I wrote dozens of letters to people and organisations I had cheated, stolen from, and lied to. Finally I felt truly free.

In *The Brothers Karamazov* Dostoevsky writes about a character who, after confessing to a murder he has kept hidden for decades, experiences the same freedom: "I feel joy and peace for the first time after so many years. There is heaven in my heart..." For the real-life murderer, "heaven" may not come so easily. Still, it should never be ruled out.

Several years ago I began to correspond with Michael Ross, a Cornell graduate turned serial rapist and killer. Given the enormity of his crimes, the terror of his victims in their last minutes, and the grief of their families, the contempt with which most people treat Michael is hardly surprising. To do anything but hate him, they feel, would be to belittle the immense suffering he has caused.

But what about Michael's own suffering? (After my first visit with him, as I embraced him and said goodbye, he broke down and wept. No one had hugged him for two decades.) What about the fact that he has been deeply remorseful for years? As he wrote in one of several letters to me:

Michael Ross

I feel a profound sense of guilt: an intense, overwhelming, and pervasive guilt that surrounds my soul with dark, tormenting clouds of self-hatred, remorse, and sorrow... Reconciliation is what I yearn for most: reconciliation with the spirit of my victims, with their families and friends, and finally with myself and God.

It is extremely unlikely that Michael will ever be forgiven by the families of his victims. It is also as good as impossible that the courts will commute his sentence from death to life imprisonment. Still, I have tried to help him see that the fate imposed on him by the law does not have to be the last word.

No matter how tortured the state of his soul, a person like Michael, who is willing to acknowledge his guilt, is far more likely to find redemption than someone whose admission has been extracted by persuasion or threats. Even if he is denied forgiveness until the day he dies, we must hope and believe that its power can touch him – if only because he yearns for it so desperately, and because he is so determined to become worthy of it.*

While it is plain that forgiveness can transform lives on a personal level, we should not forget that it can influence events on a broader scale as well. In fact, what begins as a change in one individual may affect those around him in such a way that its ripples spread wider and wider, from one person to the next.

About one hundred and fifty years ago, Möttlingen – a village in the Black Forest – experienced just such a movement. Before then, its now famous pastor, Johann Christoph Blumhardt, often sighed about the "fog of apathy" that lay over his parish. Today, aside from the streams of curious visitors that flock to see its church, the place seems equally sleepy. But a plaque on the half-timbered wall of an old house attests to remarkable events that once swept the village

*On May 13, 2005, Michael Ross was executed by lethal injection in Somers, Connecticut. He was 45.

off its feet: "Man: think on eternity, and do not mock the time of grace, for judgment is at hand!"

The "awakening" at Möttlingen, as it is referred to today, began on New Year's Eve 1843, when a young man known for his wild carousing and violent temper came to the rectory door. After pleading to see Blumhardt, he was let in. Once inside, the man confided that he hadn't slept for a whole week, and feared that he would die if he couldn't unburden his conscience. Blumhardt, somewhat cautious, remained aloof at first, but when the man began pouring out a torrent of misdeeds, large and small, he realised the confession was an earnest one.

Thus began an unprecedented wave of confessions in which one remorseful villager after another came to reveal secret sins, and to seek the relief of starting over with a clean conscience. By January 27, 1844 sixteen people had come to the rectory. Three days later, the number had risen to thirty-five. Ten days later, it stood at more than one hundred and fifty. Soon people were pouring into the parish from neighbouring villages as well.

In Möttlingen there was little of the emotionalism of most religious revivals – no exaggerated proclamations of wickedness or public avowals of repentance. What happened there was too quiet and sober for that. Pierced to the heart, people from all walks of life were suddenly able to see themselves in all their shabbiness, and felt compelled from within to break out of old ways.

Most significant, this movement went beyond words and emotions and produced concrete expressions of repentance and forgiveness. Stolen goods were returned; enemies were reconciled; infidelities were confessed and broken marriages restored. Crimes, including a case of infanticide, were solved. Even the town drunks were affected, and stayed away from the tavern.

Having travelled to Möttlingen several times over the years to visit Blumhardt's descendants (my parents, both strongly influenced by his writings, named me after him), I have often asked myself whether the awakening that took place there was merely an isolated event. But I am sure that is not the case. If the forgiveness found by one repentant man could have such far-reaching effects in his day, why shouldn't we believe that it can have equal power in ours as well?

Not a Step, but a Journey

Peter came to Jesus and said, "Master, how often shall my brother sin against me, and I forgive him? Up to seven times?" Jesus replied, "No, not up to seven times, but up to seventy times seven."

MATTHEW 18:21-22

When New York Police Department officer Steven McDonald entered Central Park on the afternoon of July 12, 1986, he had no reason to expect anything out of the ordinary. True, there had been a recent string of bicycle thefts and other petty crimes in the area, and he and his partner, Sergeant Peter King, were on the lookout. But that was a routine – all in a day's work. Then they came across a cluster of suspicious-looking teens.

> When they recognized us as cops, they cut and ran. We chased after them, my partner going in one direction and I in another. I caught up with them about thirty yards away. As I did, I said to them, "Fellas, I'm a police officer.

I'd like to talk with you." Then I asked them what their names were and where they lived. Finally I asked them, "Why are you in the park today?"

While questioning them I noticed a bulge in the pant leg of the youngest boy – it looked like he might have a gun tucked into one of his socks. I bent down to examine it. As I did, I felt someone move over me, and as I looked up, the taller of the three (he turned out to be 15) was pointing a gun at my head. Before I knew what was happening, there was a deafening explosion, the muzzle flashed, and a bullet struck me above my right eye. I remember the reddish-orange flame that jumped from the barrel, the smell of the gunpowder, and the smoke. I fell backward, and the boy shot me a second time, hitting me in the throat. Then, as I lay on the ground, he stood over me and shot me a third time.

I was in pain; I was numb; I knew I was dying, and I didn't want to die. It was terrifying. My partner was yelling into his police radio: "Ten Thirteen Central! Ten Thirteen!" and when I heard that code, I knew I was in a very bad way. Then I closed my eyes...

Steven doesn't remember what happened next, but when the first officers to respond arrived on the scene, they found Sergeant King sitting on the ground, covered in Steven's blood, cradling him in his arms and rocking him back and forth. He was crying. Knowing that every wasted second could be fatal, the men heaved Steven into the back of their police car and rushed him to the nearest emergency room, at Harlem's

Metropolitan Hospital, twenty blocks away. Immediately paramedics, nurses, and doctors went to work. For the next forty-eight hours, he hung between life and death. At one point, Steven's chief surgeon even told the police commissioner, "He's not going to make it. Call the family. Tell them to come say goodbye." But then he turned a corner.

> They did the impossible: they saved me, but my wounds were devastating. The bullet that struck my throat had hit my spine, and I couldn't move my arms or legs, or breathe without a ventilator. In less than a second, I had gone from being an active police officer to an incapable crime victim. I was paralysed from the neck down.
>
> When the surgeon came into my room to tell me this, my wife, Patti Ann, was there, and he told her I would need to be institutionalised. We had been married just eight months, and Patti Ann, who was 23 at the time, was three months pregnant. She collapsed to the floor, crying uncontrollably. I cried too, though I was locked in my body, and unable to move or to reach out to her.

Steven spent the next eighteen months in the hospital, first in New York and then in Colorado. It was like learning to live all over again, this time completely dependent on other people. There were endless things to get used to – being fed, bathed, and helped to the toilet.

> Then, about six months after I was shot, Patti Ann gave birth to a baby boy. We named him Conor. To me, Conor's

birth was like a message from God that I should live, and live differently. And it was clear to me that I had to respond to that message. I prayed that I would be changed, that the person I was would be replaced by something new.

That prayer was answered with a desire to forgive the young man who shot me. I wanted to free myself of all the negative, destructive emotions that his act of violence had unleashed in me: anger, bitterness, hatred, and other feelings. I needed to free myself of those emotions so that I could love my wife and our child and those around us.

Then, shortly after Conor's birth, we held a press conference. People wanted to know what I was thinking and how I was doing. That's when Patti Ann told everyone that I had forgiven the young man who tried to kill me.

Steven and his assailant, whose name was Shavod Jones, could not have been more different. Steven was white; Shavod was black. Steven came from the middle-class suburbs of Long Island's Nassau County; Shavod from a Harlem housing project. Their brief encounter might have ended right there. But Steven wouldn't let it. Knowing that his attacker had just altered the course of both of their lives, he felt an uncanny connection to him:

Strangely, we became friends. It began with my writing to him. At first he didn't answer my letters, but then he wrote back. Then one night a year or two later, he called my home from prison and apologised to my wife, my son, and me. We accepted his apology, and I told him I hoped he and I could work together in the future. I hoped that one day we might travel around the country together sharing how this act of violence had changed both our lives, and how it had given us an understanding of what is most important in life.

Eventually the exchange fizzled out. Then, in late 1995, Shavod was released from prison. Three days later, he was killed in a motorcycle accident. Others might feel Steven's efforts to reach out to his attacker were wasted, but he himself doesn't think so:

> I was a badge to that kid, a uniform representing the government. I was the system that let landlords charge rent for squalid apartments in broken-down tenements; I was the city agency that fixed up poor neighbourhoods and drove the residents out, through gentrification, regardless of whether they were law-abiding solid citizens, or pushers and criminals; I was the Irish cop who showed up at a domestic dispute and left without doing anything, because no law had been broken.
>
> To Shavod Jones, I was the enemy. He didn't see me as a person, as a man with loved ones, as a husband and father-to-be. He'd bought into all the stereotypes of his community: the police are racist, they'll turn violent, so arm yourself against them. And I couldn't blame him. Society – his family, the social agencies responsible for him, the people who'd made it impossible for his parents to be together – had failed him way before he had met me in Central Park.

Steven and Patti Ann and Conor McDonald

When visiting Steven in his Long Island home (since meeting in 1997, we have become close friends), I am often struck by the extent of his incapacitation. Life in a wheelchair is hard enough for an elderly person to accept, but to be plucked out of an active, fun-loving life in your prime is devastating. Add to that a tracheostomy to breathe through and total dependence on a nurse and other caregivers, and life can seem pretty confining at times. Steven is matter-of-fact about this:

> There's nothing easy about being paralysed. I have not been able to hold my wife in my arms for two decades. Conor is now a young man, and I've never been able to have a catch with him. It's frustrating – difficult – ugly – at times.

So why did he forgive? Again, he himself says it best:

> I forgave Shavod because I believe the only thing worse than receiving a bullet in my spine would have been to nurture revenge in my heart. Such an attitude would have extended my injury to my soul, hurting my wife, son, and others even more. It's bad enough that the physical effects are permanent, but at least I can choose to prevent spiritual injury.
>
> Again, I have my ups and downs. Some days, when I am not feeling very well, I can get angry. I get depressed. There have been times when I even felt like killing myself. But I have come to realise that anger is a wasted emotion...
>
> Of course, I didn't forgive Shavod right away. It took time. Things have evolved over fourteen years. I think about it almost every day. But I can say this: I've never regretted forgiving him.

Patti Ann feels the same:

> It's been hard, very hard, for me to *really* forgive the boy that shot Steven. Why did he have to do it? I still want to know. Why couldn't my son grow up having the same experiences other kids have with their dads? We still struggle over that one. But I learned long ago that in order for us to get along as a couple, I had to let go of my anger. Otherwise Steven and I wouldn't have been able to go on ourselves. Because when something like that festers inside of you, it just destroys you from the inside out.

Today, Steven is a sought-after speaker at schools in and around New York City, holding entire auditoriums captive as he retells his story and launches dialogue on the broader issues surrounding it. To him, the cycle of violence that plagues so many lives today – including young lives, like that of Shavod – can be overcome only by breaking down the walls that separate people and make them afraid of each other. The best tools for this, he says, are love, respect, and forgiveness.

Quoting Robert F. Kennedy, Steven likes to point out that "the victims of violence are black and white, rich and poor, young and old, famous and unknown, but they are, most important of all, human beings whom other human beings have loved and needed." And somewhere in each address, he finds a way to refer to Martin Luther King – a man who gives him unending inspiration:

> When I was a very young kid, Dr. King came to my town in New York. My mother went to hear him speak, and she was very impressed by what she heard. I hope you can be inspired by his words too. Dr. King said that there's some good in the worst of us, and some evil in the best of us, and that when we learn this, we'll be more loving and forgiving. He also said, "Forgiveness is not an occasional act, it's a permanent attitude." In other words, it is something you have to work for. Just like you have to work to keep your body fit and your mind alert, you've got to work on your heart too. Forgiving is not just a one-time decision. You've got to *live* forgiveness, every day.

If Steven's story illustrates the ongoing battle that follows every decision to forgive, the next one, about an eight-year-old girl named Saira Sher, shows how that battle cannot be won without a decisive first step.

Saira was three when she was hit by a car while walking across a street in Troy, New York with her mother. Months of surgery, recuperation, and therapy followed, but she never fully recovered.

Today, despite her confinement to a wheelchair and her inability to walk or use her arms and hands (she writes by holding a pen between her teeth), Saira is a spunky nine-year old who has dreams of becoming lead vocalist in her own rock band and founding a home for disabled children. "I'm trapped outside, but free on the inside," she wrote in a recent issue of her school newspaper. "I probably do more than anyone else that can walk. Over all, being paralysed isn't so bad."

But if you talk to grandmother (and primary caregiver) Alice Calonga, you'll get another angle of the picture:

> Saira's an inspiration. She doesn't have any animosity at all. She is a very positive human being, and doesn't dwell on what happened to her or feel sorry for herself. She's just a normal kid, as far as she's concerned. As much as was taken from her, she's given that much back a thousand times in her short life to the people around her. But that still doesn't undo what was done to her...

I'll never forget the first couple of days after the accident. We were up in Albany in the paediatric ICU and there were a lot of people milling around with their children. But there were two young men there who kind of stood out, because they were always there, watching me. Finally one of them approached me and asked me if I was related to the little girl who got hit by the car. I said I was. Then he asked me if I was her grandmother. I said yes.

At this point I asked him who he was, and he said he was the man who had hit her. I was stunned. Then he asked me if I could forgive him. When I tried to put myself in this stranger's shoes and think how devastated I would feel if I were him, I right away knew I had to forgive him. So I did. Then I hugged him.

Just at that moment my daughter came out of the ICU. She was horrified to see me talking with this man and was very angry at me.

She started telling me how the accident had happened – how the driver had been so impatient, he had driven around the vehicle in front of him, which had stopped for a traffic light, and run into her and Saira. Then, trying to flee the scene, he had accelerated and hit Saira a second time, breaking her neck and crushing her spine.

At first I couldn't believe it. I said, "Nobody would do anything like that." But I soon found out that my daughter was not exaggerating. I was so horrified, I felt like I had been raped. I had been robbed of my forgiveness by a man who wasn't the least bit entitled to it...

Saira Sher

Alice says that despite her shock – and the fury of her daughter, who told her she had no right to forgive anyone for what happened – she is certain she did the right thing.

As angry as some people are that I did it, in my heart I know I forgave that driver for the right reason, even if I was just going on instinct. I can honestly say that if I had not forgiven him at that particular moment, I might never have been able to. It's so clear to me now that he didn't deserve it. But if I were him – if I had done what he did – I know I would still want forgiveness. That's how I was thinking when I originally forgave him.

Of course, since then I've found out a lot more about that driver. He's continued to flout the law and to do bodily harm to others without showing any kind of remorse. Last I heard he had thirty-seven violations on his license! When he hit Saira he already had nineteen. Lord only knows what else he has done.

Alice says it's a daily fight to hang on to her initial offer of forgiveness. But she also says that the struggle has made her a stronger person.

It's taken me such a long time to get over the feeling of having been used. A long time. But I *have* gotten over it. I don't think he'll ever be worthy of my forgiveness. Still, I can carry my burdens a whole lot easier now, than when I had to carry my anger around as well. And because of that I can live a better life and give my energy to someone who deserves it – someone like Saira.

By illustrating the power of forgiveness in their own lives, people like Steven and Alice make exemplary models for others who want to forgive. But ultimately they are just that: models. And if their stories are to be of any real use beyond merely edifying us, we must find the points at which their journeys intersect with our own.

Obviously, the road to healing and wholeness cannot be the same for everyone. Every person moves at his or her own pace, and there are different paths to the same destination. Some people find strength to forgive within themselves, others through the help of those around them. Some are able to forgive only when they recognize their own inadequacy and turn to a higher power. Still others are never really able to forgive at all.

Terry, a local prison inmate I correspond with, is thirty-seven years old. So far he's spent nineteen of them in prisons, jails, or detention homes of one kind or another. Forcibly abducted from his abusive parents by child welfare agents determined to save him and his siblings, Terry and his brothers were shunted from one foster home to another over a period of two decades.

In one foster home Terry was severely beaten by the woman in charge; at another, repeatedly raped by older roommates. In yet another home, the priest who ran it molested him. Multiple escapes were followed by multiple recaptures, which were followed by days of solitary confinement in a locked room, his food passed through a slot in the door, and nothing to wear but undershorts.

Terry has spent so much of his life on drugs and alcohol that parts of his youth are only a blur. He has attempted suicide too many times to count. Still, he yearns to forgive the people who have made his life the hell it is, to forgive himself for the "stupid choices" he recognises that he himself made along the way, and to be forgiven for the crimes (burglary and drunk driving) that have landed him in jail.

I'll sit and tell you every one of my sins, and I am truly very sorry for every one, even for the ones I'm not even aware of. Believe me, I've got a good heart. I'd give whatever I have if someone asked me. I love other people but hate myself. Does that make any sense? It hurts me to see someone else hurt, but at the same time I've hurt every person I ever loved. Are all my emotions directed in the wrong places, or am I just a real screwball?

To be honest, a lot of my problems have to do with holding on to grudges. I do not know how to let them go. There's so much pent-up anger in me, so much hate and bitterness inside, I'm just not able to truly love. Nothing seems to be able to block the demons in my head or take away the unexplained pain I feel each and every day.

When I'm with other people, I can fake it. I joke around, I laugh. But once I'm alone, I get sober, and all these feelings – loneliness, abandonment, revenge, suicide – come welling up and take hold of me. I've undergone psychiatric counselling; I've been through rehab and halfway houses. I've been on every medication there is. But nothing works for me. Nothing.

I've begged Jesus to come into my life so many times, and part of him has, or I wouldn't be writing this letter to you. But how do I get rid of all the crap that takes up so much space in my mind? I feel like I'm unable to make a conscious decision to stop hating...

My childhood is over and done, I know, but I am still pissed off at my parents because of what they did to me and my brothers when we were kids. Sometimes I lie in bed at night dreaming about how I'd punch them in the face if I ever saw them again. I know the Bible says, "Honour your father and mother." But I can't. I try to. I try very hard. But I just can't let my anger go. I am so messed up by my childhood. Last time I saw my oldest brother, he was dying of AIDS. Another brother has been in a mental hospital for forty years now. Another lives upstate and beats the hell out of his children, like Dad beat the hell out of him. I've called the child protection agency on him several times...

I pray for forgiveness. I pray for other people. I pray that God can help me to become the person he wants me to be. I pray that I can accept anything thrown at me in the course of a day. I pray that I can accept who I am.

I need to learn how to rid myself of the hate I feel, because it's killing me. One of my biggest fears is dying in this prison. I'm scared my soul would be stuck here.

I honestly want to forgive those I hate – including my parents – even though dark thoughts enter my mind all the time, and I have to pray daily to remove them. I see my own need for forgiveness too. I want so badly to be a good person and to change my ways.

I've read in the Bible about how Jesus touched people and transformed their lives. They only had to get close enough to him to touch his robe, and then they'd be healed. I know I'm only a speck of dust among millions of others, but I wish I could find that healing for myself. Or am I expecting too much?

Terry may never be able to confront the people who need his forgiveness, or come to terms with the suffering he has endured at their hands. Even if he did, he might never be able to pull himself together and verbalise the forgiveness he wishes he could grant them. In a situation like his, where the fear of being misunderstood or trampled on is very great, it may be too painful to expose one's deepest feelings.

In the end, however, it is not words that matter. For Terry, as for each of us, it is our inmost attitude that really counts. That is what will tip the scales of our lives in the direction we really want to go, no matter how many conflicting emotions threaten to throw us off balance.

When Bud Welch lost his 23-year-old daughter Julie, he lost the pride of his life, and to this day he cannot say he has forgiven the man who killed her. Still, he refuses to give resentment and despair the upper hand, and tries instead to keep her memory alive by sharing his pride in her with others.

> I'm the third of eight children and grew up on a dairy farm, and I've run a service station in Oklahoma City for the last thirty-four years. Until April 19, 1995 – the day Julie and 167 others were killed in the bomb blast that destroyed the Alfred P. Murrah Building – my life was very simple. I had a little girl and loved her a lot.

Bud Welch

Julie had a rough start; she was born premature, but she survived and grew healthy and strong. She had just graduated from Marquette with a degree in Spanish and started a job as a translator for the Social Security Administration. At the time of her death she was dating an Air Force lieutenant named Eric. The day after Julie was killed I found out that they had decided to announce their engagement in two weeks.

All my life I have opposed the death penalty. Friends used to tell me that if anyone ever killed one of my family members, I would change. "What if Julie got raped and murdered?" But I always said I'd stick to my guns. Until April 19.

The first four or five weeks after the bombing I had so much anger, pain, hatred, and revenge, that I realised why, when someone is charged with a violent crime, they transport him in a bullet-proof vest. It's because people like me would try to kill him.

By the end of 1995 I was in such bad shape, I was drinking heavily and smoking three packs of cigarettes a day. I was stuck, emotionally, on April 19. I just couldn't get over it. But I knew I had to do something about it. That's when I went down to the bombing site.

It was a cold January afternoon, and I stood there watching hundreds of people walking along the chain link fence that surrounded the lot where the Murrah Building had stood. I was thinking about the death penalty, and how I wanted nothing more than to see Timothy McVeigh (and anyone else responsible for the bombing) fried. But I was also beginning to wonder whether I would really feel any better once they were executed. Every time I asked myself that question, I got the same answer: No. Nothing positive would come from it. It wouldn't bring Julie back. After all, it was hatred and revenge that made me want to see them dead, and those two things were the very reason that Julie and 167 others were dead...

Once he arrived at this realisation, Bud returned to his original belief that executing criminals was wrong, and he has since become a leading opponent of the death penalty. Sought across the country as a speaker on the futility of capital punishment, he makes appearances in churches and town meetings, on college campuses and at activist gatherings. He is always on the go. But nothing he has done means as much to him as his meeting with Timothy's father:

A person like Bill McVeigh is as much a victim as I am, if not more. I can't imagine the pain he and his family have been through. I've lost a daughter, and if Timothy is ever executed he's going to lose a son. I have a son myself, and if he was convicted of killing 168 people, I don't know how I'd deal with that. Bill has to live with that for the rest of his life.

I first saw Bill McVeigh on television a few weeks after the bombing. He was working in his flower bed, and he looked up at the camera for a couple seconds. When he did I saw a father with deep, deep pain in his eyes. I could recognise it, because I was living that pain. I knew right then that someday I had to go tell him that I truly cared how he felt.

So I did. The day I visited him he was out in his garden again, and we spent about half an hour just getting acquainted, kicking dirt and pulling weeds. Then we went into the house so I could meet Jennifer, his 24-year-old daughter. As we walked in I noticed a few family photos on the wall over the kitchen table. The largest one was of Timothy. I kept glancing up at that picture. I knew that they were watching me, so I said, "Gosh, what a good-looking kid." Bill had told me outdoors that he was having a lot of trouble showing emotion – that he couldn't cry. But when I commented on that photograph he said, "That's Tim's high school graduation picture," and a great big tear rolled down his cheek.

We talked for another hour and a half. When I got ready to leave I shook Bill's hand and extended my hand to Jennifer. She didn't take it. She hugged me around the neck. I don't know who started crying first as we embraced, but we were both in tears. Finally I said, "Honey, we're in this together for the rest of our lives. And we can make the most of it, if we choose. I don't want your brother to die, and I'll do everything in my power to prevent it." Never in my life have I felt closer to God than I did at that time. I felt like a thousand pounds had been lifted off my shoulders.

Still, Bud says he has no desire to meet his daughter's killer. Sometimes he's not even sure he's really forgiven him:

> ...At least I don't think I have forgiven him. I was speaking at Oklahoma State University one time, and the Bishop of Tulsa was there. I was telling the group about my struggle, and that I didn't feel that I had forgiven him. Anyway, the bishop chimed in and said, "But I think you *have* forgiven him." And he started quoting some verse from Scripture, which I'm not very good at doing. But he's a bishop, and I suppose he's qualified. I guess he was trying to convince me that I have forgiven Timothy, and maybe I have.
>
> I still have my moments of rage. I remember crossing the campus of a high school in California, on my way to speak to an all-school assembly, and looking around as I walked. The place reminded me of Julie's high school. Suddenly this rage just hit me. So here I was, getting ready to speak to a whole auditorium full of kids about my opposition to the death penalty, and I was thinking to myself, "That bastard doesn't even deserve to live."
>
> I know I don't want Timothy executed, because once he's gone, it will be too late to choose to forgive him.* As long as he's alive, I have to deal with my feelings and emo-

tions. But I do have setbacks, even when I'm sure I want to forgive. That's probably why I can't handle that word "closure." I get sick of hearing it. The first time someone asked me about closure was the day after Julie's burial. Of course I was still in hell then. In a way, I still am. How can there ever be true closure? A part of my heart is gone.

Bud has been an inspiration to me from the very first time we met, and each time I see him, I sense an increased determination to make the best he can of the tragedy that hit him. While it was grief that first led him to visit the family of his daughter's killer, it is her life-affirming spirit that drives him now. And even if he hasn't yet found the full measure of healing he seeks, his journey – like every journey of forgiveness – is one of hope:

> It's a struggle, but it's one I need to wage. In any case, forgiving is not something you just wake up one morning and decide to do. You have to work through your anger and your hatred as long as it's there. You try to live each day a little better than the one before.

*Over Bud Welch's protests, Timothy McVeigh was executed by lethal injection on June 11, 2001, in Terre Haute, Indiana.

Making Ripples

Love in action is a harsh and dreadful thing compared with love in dreams. Love in dreams is greedy for immediate action, rapidly performed and in sight of all. Men will give their lives if only the ordeal does not last long…with all looking on and applauding. But active love is labour and fortitude.

FYODOR DOSTOEVSKY

For years, whenever I heard the name *Rwanda,* my reaction was almost instantaneous. The word *genocide* jumped to mind, and with it, horrifying images from 1994, when whole villages were wiped out in one of the worst mass-killings in recent history. Today, hearing the same name, a very different word comes to mind: *forgiveness,* and its capacity to redeem even the darkest chapters of human history. The change in my reaction came in 2008, after meeting Jean-Paul Samputu.

A world-class musician with a busy concert schedule, Jean-Paul has been compared to Paul Simon, and sung everywhere from rural Africa to New York City's Lincoln Centre. He has won numerous honours, including the prestigious Kora Award. But it wasn't his music that caught my attention. It was his journey from anger and hatred to forgiveness and joy...

Think about it: one *million* people were murdered in ninety days! Friends killed friends, brothers killed brothers, sisters killed sisters, and children killed their parents. Parents killed their children, and husbands killed their wives...

Meanwhile, I was touring in Burundi and Uganda – I was well known in Rwanda, and my father had advised me to flee. But I came back in July 1994, at the end of the genocide.

I already knew that my parents were dead – they had been killed in Butare, our home village south of the capital, in May. Three of my brothers had also been killed, and my 34-year-old sister. It was horrible.

My family is Tutsi, and our neighbours were killing our people. But since my sister was married to a Hutu, I thought she would be safe. She wasn't. They killed her little by little, over three days. There are many things I am not able to talk about...

When I got back to Rwanda, I travelled to Butare, and went to my father's house. It was empty. I looked for the neighbours. There was no one around. There were bodies everywhere. And the smell! Eventually I found some survivors, and learned who had killed my parents. It was my best childhood friend, Vincent. We had grown up together, played soccer together. I was stunned; it totally destroyed me.

Virtually everybody – every Tutsi – lost family members in 1994. But to think that my parents had been killed by my best friend! I lost my mind. I started to drink and use drugs. I would drink a whole bottle of *waragi*, an African gin, every day. I used to wonder why I didn't die. Now I know.

For the next nine years I lived in a daze. The anger, pain, and bitterness was totally devastating. There was a war going on in me, tearing me apart. I couldn't sing any more because I was always drunk. I couldn't honour contracts; I was never ready to go on stage.

I went to Uganda, and friends tried to help me. They brought me to one witch doctor after another, but nothing helped. I was angry with myself, and with God. "Where were you, God?" I asked over and over. "How could you permit such things to happen?"

Around this time my wife had a child, Claudia. The baby was severely disabled. That made me even angrier. I blamed God. It destroyed us to have that child, and my wife and I accused each other...

In 1998 the Samputus moved to Canada. They settled in Montreal, home to a sizeable community of Rwandan immigrants, and had another child. In 2000, they separated. Jean-Paul returned to Africa.

I went to Uganda – I was a star there – and put on a big concert. I made money again. But because of my drinking and drugging, I kept landing up in prison. I was in and out, in and out. I know all the prisons there: I did time in all of them.

Finally one of my brothers paid a lot of money to have me released, and I went to join him in Kenya, where he lived. While I was there, a friend of his wife's family, an evangelist named Moses, visited. He said he had come because of me – that God had told him to find me and pray for me.

I was hesitant, but I listened, and then I let him pray over me. To be honest, I was ready for anything at this point. I didn't have any choice. Nothing else had worked.

Moses' prayers were powerful. He helped me overcome my alcoholism and drug addiction by commanding the demons to leave me. He prayed, "Come out of him, in the name of Jesus." Whenever he said the name of Jesus, I felt something strange. Often I fell down, and sometimes I would even vomit. It is hard to describe. All I can say is that when this man prayed, it was unbelievably powerful.

At first, I told him, "You are the best of the best witch doctors." (That was the only thing I knew.) He laughed: "No, I am not a witch doctor." And when I thanked him, he insisted he had done nothing but pray. "Don't thank me. I am not your healer. It is Jesus." Soon I was longing for Jesus. I wanted to find out more about *him,* who he was. Three months later I stopped drinking, I stopped doing drugs.

In 2003 I went back to Uganda. I was now a Christian, and all the newspapers wrote about it, just like they had earlier when I had gone to prison. It was a big story: "Samputu changes his life." "Samputu believes in prayer." I went to Sseguku, Uganda's famous Mountain of Prayer. People go there from all over to be with God. I spent three months alone there, trying to find Jesus.

On Sseguku I prayed and prayed, and asked God all my questions. I always received the same answer. It would come to me in dreams, through a voice that I seemed to be talking with. This happened night after night, and the message was always the same: You have to forgive.

I used to go to a church on the mountain, and there I would find the same thing being preached. I did not want to hear it, but it was inescapable. Again and again, I would hear this voice telling me, in my sleep, "You will be healed only when you forgive." But I kept resisting for at least another year.

Again, I was Christian: I had stopped drinking. I was no longer doing drugs. But I was not fully delivered or healed. I was "okay," but there was still bitterness deep inside me. And that was the problem. Because it is not enough to be a Christian, or even to know the whole Bible. That's only half the programme. The important thing is to live what you know – to live the truth.

For me this meant one thing: I had to repent and go pay the debts I had everywhere. I had to ask forgiveness for where I had hurt others. I had to forgive Vincent, and I had to forgive my wife.

It was a hard battle. I kept saying No. No! It took months. Then one day it all became too much. I had to give in, to say Yes. I told myself, "I'm ready, right now, to forgive Vincent." With that, I was delivered – totally healed, and freed from everything in my past. I had peace in my heart. All this, just because I had finally said Yes to that voice. I called my wife. I went to look for Vincent. He was in prison, but I found his wife, Regina, and told her to tell Vincent I had forgiven him...

When I asked Jean-Paul to pinpoint what made him forgive his old friend, he said he had been worried that he himself was turning into a murderer:

It's a good thing I didn't find Vincent before I did. I had never harmed another person, but in my head, it was what I planned to do. I was going to kill him. And if I hadn't been able to do it myself, I was going to ask someone else to do it for me. That's where hatred leads: you end up becoming a killer yourself, even if you don't have any idea how to kill.

When I did finally forgive Vincent, he had trouble believing me. He said to his wife, "How on earth can he do this? After what I did?" He was sure it was a trick, a political ploy. But his wife told him, "I have talked with Samputu. If you don't accept his forgiveness, that's your problem. But let me tell you one thing. It's not *him* who's forgiving you. It's God. It's grace."

In the end, Vincent believed me, and this brought about a remarkable thing. Earlier, his wife would not allow him back into the house. She couldn't see living with an unrepentant killer. But after Vincent accepted my forgiveness (he saw that it was really God) he was able to repent and to forgive himself. And after that, Regina also forgave him. She said, "If God can forgive you through Samputu, I should be able to forgive you too." And their children also forgave him. He is now at home. The family is together. When I go there I eat with them. That's how the power of forgiveness works.

Jean-Paul's transformation also brought his own family together again. In 2005, he rejoined his wife and children in Canada.

Since then many miracles have happened in my life. God spoke through our disabled daughter's caregiver, and showed us that she was not a cripple but an angel. She said, "God created Claudia, and in his eyes there is nothing wrong with her. You feel bad that you have such a child. You don't even want to look at her. You should be proud of her."

The next time I went to see Claudia (she is not able to live with us, but lives in a special facility), I cried, and my son saw me crying. "Why you crying?" he asked. Then we prayed with her. I could finally say, "God gave me this child."

Through Claudia's caregiver, I came to feel that I am blessed to have such a daughter. And today, instead of accusing each other for our child's condition, my wife and I know what a treasure she is. Now I know why I didn't

Vincent Ntkirutimana and Jean-Paul Samputu

die when I was trying to kill myself with drugs and drink. God saved me to be a father.

As Jean-Paul's story (and almost every other in this book) bears out, forgiving is a deeply personal matter. Ultimately each of us must find healing within, on our own terms, and in our own time. On another level, however, forgiving is much more. Even if it initially connects people one by one, the resulting "ripple effect" can be felt on a much broader scale. In fact, forgiveness can be a powerful social force, transforming and empowering whole groups of people.

Historically, Martin Luther King's role in the Civil Rights Movement, and Gandhi's in India's struggle for independence, are the most familiar examples of this. But there are plenty of others. Volumes could be written about South Africa's Truth and Reconciliation Commission, and the hearings it organised in the mid-1990s. Under its guidance, hundreds of victims and perpetrators of the country's brutal apartheid policies came forward to face the past, in hopes of redeeming it and building a more stable society.

In 1999 (and again in 2000) my wife and I travelled through Northern Ireland as participants in a special "Journey for Peace" and met hundreds of adults – and even more inspiring, hundreds of children there – who had come together to heal the wounds of the region's so-called Troubles by promoting dialogue and reconciliation between Catholic and Protestant citizens.

Almost ten years later, the same thing is happening in Rwanda. Take Nyamata, for example, a town south of Kigali. When the genocide began in the spring of 1994, Mukamana, a Tutsi teen, and Aziri, a Hutu farmer, found themselves in opposite camps.

Returning from the well one April day, Mukamana found that her entire family had been hacked to death with machetes. She hid in a field, and later fled to Burundi.

Aziri, the farmer, did not take part in this particular massacre, but later confessed to killing others in the area.

Today, the two are neighbours again, and even go to the same church on Sundays. "We help each other," Aziri told a reporter from IRIN, a news service affiliated with the United Nations. "When a member of one family is sick, we drop by." Even more significant, he says, "Our kids are friends."

Along with about forty other families in Nyamata, Mukamana and Aziri are members of a community where genocide survivors and confessed perpetrators live side by side. The settlement, which they call Imidugudo ("reconciliation village") was started by Steven Gahigi, an Anglican clergyman whose mother, father and siblings were all killed in 1994.

Gahigi thought he had lost his ability to forgive: "I prayed until one night I saw an image of Jesus Christ on the cross...I thought of how he forgave, and I knew that I and others could also do it." Inspired by his vision, Gahigi began preaching forgiveness. He did this not only in Nyamata, but in the prisons where Hutu perpetrators sat awaiting trial. (Thousands were released by the government in 2003, to relieve overcrowding.)

Learning to forgive has not been easy, the villagers say. "For a long time I did not think I could ever forgive," Mukamana admits. But wherever people are willing to face the past honestly, old wounds can be healed, and amazing things can happen. That is what seems to make forgiveness possible in Imidugudo, where pe

own children about their roles in 19

mous consequences both for those wh

who survived," says Xavier Namay, an ad

"My children must know what I did so the

country positively."

Similar initiatives have popped up elsew

the globe in recent years. From Israel to Indo ...a, from

Baghdad to the Balkans, groups like Christian Peacemaker

Teams, the American Friends Service Committee, and

other nongovernmental organisations are promoting rec-

onciliation as the only way to overcome ethnic strife. In

most cases, their achievements are modest, given the scope

of the problems they are tackling. Victories are often fol-

lowed by setbacks, and by accusations of unfounded opti-

mism or idealism. In Rwanda, for instance, where I attended

a conference on forgiving in February 2009, I met plenty of

people who are giving their energies to build a new society

built on love and trust. But they are still far outnumbered

by people who claim that reconciliation is an empty dream.

Some of these people openly promote the old ideologies

that led to genocide. In the face of such realities, Jean-Paul

is matter of fact:

> It's true that the cycle of violence often seems endless. Each
> incident produces another. Each person or group of peo-
> ple seems to have their own enemy. Ironically, those "en-

often not even around anymore. In many cases, re not even alive. To me, the *real* enemy is one we all face: the anger and bitterness we carry around with us during the day; the fear and anxiety we sleep with at night. We don't need other people! We are killing ourselves.

People are still imprisoned: by fear, anger, mistrust, suspicion, and revenge. There is still bitterness and resentment, and the racist theories that led to the mass killings of 1994 are still being taught in our schools. People who spent years behind bars are now coming home, and if you meet one of them – if you meet somebody who killed your cousin, your uncle, or your mother, and you talk with him – you can't talk like you did before. It's impossible, without love. Only love can deliver us from old hatreds and bondages and bring about true healing.

People all over the world are hurting like this – not just in Rwanda. Tragically, they act as if there is no way out. They say, "Things happen." "That's the way life is." They won't talk about the solution, which is forgiveness. Only a culture of forgiveness can stop the cycle of violence and despair and set into motion new cycles of hope and love.

This will not happen overnight, because forgiving is a very personal choice. It takes soul-searching. People need to be shown why they should go to all the trouble. They need to hear stories of forgiveness, so that they can be touched. And they need a vision of how things could be, in order to give them hope.

Such a vision is the essence of an old freedom song I remember from the sixties, which went, "One man's hands can't break a prison down / Two men's hands can't break a prison down / But if two and two and fifty make a million / We'll see that day come 'round..." This is the hope that has led victims and perpetrators of "ethnic cleansing" in a handful of villages in Kosovo to come together and till the soil in communal gardens; it is what prompted Christian survivors of Muslim persecution in 1998–1999 in the Maluka Islands of Indonesia to forgive those who burned their homes and raped their wives and daughters.

It is also what continues to inspire other creative impulses around the world, such as a theatre project in Pittsburgh in the summer of 2008 which brought together Israeli Jews, Arab Muslims, and American Christians to build community. Using "playback," a dramatic form that encourages story-telling, potential antagonists were invited to imagine walking in each other's shoes, and to bat around new solutions, rather than just rehash old problems. (Afterward, participants planned to take what they learned back home, for use as a peacemaking tool.)

"There's so much fear, misunderstanding and hurt," says Roni Ostfield, the director of the project. "And it's real pain. But our hope is always that if one person's heart is open to communication with the other side, maybe that person can touch ten other people, and it can grow from there."

And why shouldn't it? The anthropologist Margaret Mead once admonished, we should "never doubt that a

small group of committed people can change the world...
Indeed, it's the only thing that ever has." Mead's words rang
true in a new way a few years ago, in the wake of the so-
called Amish School Massacre.

On October 2, 2006, a milk-truck driver named Charles
Roberts walked, unannounced, into a one-room Amish
school near his home in eastern Pennsylvania and ordered
the boys and the teacher to leave. After tying the legs of the
remaining girls, Roberts prepared to shoot them execution-
style, with an automatic rifle and four hundred rounds of
ammunition that he brought for the task.

The oldest girl, a thirteen-year-old, begged Roberts to
"shoot me first and let the little ones go." Refusing her offer,
he opened fire on all of them, killing five and leaving the
others critically wounded. He then shot himself as police
stormed the building.

No one may ever know his real motive, but Roberts apparently told the children in the school that he was angry
at God for taking his little daughter, who had died as a baby
several years earlier.

Within hours, the story captured the attention of news
media around the world. By evening, television crews had
clogged the small village of Nickel Mines. They stayed for
almost a week, until the killer and the victims were buried.

Brutal as it was, the massacre itself was soon eclipsed by a remarkable second chapter to the story: the forgiving attitude of the families who had lost their daughters. In fact, the blood was barely dry on the schoolhouse floor when members of this deeply religious community approached the parents and the widow of the gunman to offer their sympathy and to ask how they were doing. It went beyond talk – the Amish even set up a fund for the shooter's widow and her children. Food, too, was collected for the gunman's family. On the same day of the massacre, a reporter came across an Amish man making the rounds of several local farms, gathering donations. Most surprising, grieving families accounted for about half of the people who attended the killer's burial, during which they again reached out to his widow, Marie, and her three children.

"Outsiders" generally admire the Amish, but in this case, many found their response to the killings hard to believe. As one TV anchor said, "All religions teach forgiveness. But no one really does it, like the Amish are trying to. What is the difference?"

I don't think it was easy for the Amish to forgive. I know many, and I have friends who know some of the affected families. They are no saintlier than others: indeed, for them, as for most people, forgiving was not a one-time decision. It took struggle and recommitment, sometimes daily. One of the victims spent months in a coma; others were brain-damaged, and will always require special nursing care. Some of the families are so fearful that they are still schooling their children at home. Everyone involved will be dealing with the residue of that horrifying morning for the rest of their lives.

But as far as open anger or hostility goes, the Amish hold, as they have for centuries, that it is destructive – a waste of energy that will hold them hostage and ultimately kill them, just like their daughters were held hostage and killed by someone else's anger. To these devout followers of Jesus, the only answer is the one he offered on the Cross: "Father, forgive them, for they know not what they do."

Jesus' attitude is not a popular one in our day, even in religious quarters. And in the rare instances where it is promoted publicly, the response is often sceptical, if not downright cynical. Such was the case in 2005, when the Serbian Orthodox Church surprised observers across Europe by asking forgiveness for its support of Milosevic's regime. "We honestly offer our Albanian co-citizens reconciliation and mutual forgiveness," it said in the opening sentence of a public statement.

Critics belittled the apology as a political move, but there were others who embraced the chance for dialogue. They noted that whatever its effect, it was the first such attempt to honestly address the hatreds that had led to one atrocity after another across the region for most of the previous decade.

Naysayers similarly questioned the sincerity of Australian Prime Minister Kevin Rudd when, in early 2008, he made a public apology to his country's aboriginal peoples for the government's longstanding policies of racial segregation, containment, and de facto abuse. Others welcomed the Prime Minister's words. One was Fr. Michael Lapsley of South Africa:

> Of course, an apology does not take away the truth of the wrong that was done and the pain that continues to be felt through the generations by indigenous Australians. Nevertheless there is no doubt that this representative acknowledgment...can be balm in the wounds, a major step and a turning point on the long journey towards restorative justice and healing for all...
>
> Over the years I have heard many of you speak about your own sense of guilt and shame about what happened in your country's history. Today I am sure that many of you shed tears of joy that finally the day has come in a dignified way to squarely face the horror of what happened and to travel a new journey.

Fr. Lapsley was not responding as a mere observer. Persecuted by the South African government for fighting apartheid, this activist priest and internationally-known advocate of "restorative justice" had been banned from the country and then lost both hands and an eye in a parcel bomb explosion. Since then, he has worked with victims of torture and founded Cape Town's Institute of Healing Memories, where he has counselled hundreds of survivors of violence. He realised that an apology – any apology – is singularly important because it often represents the first crucial step without which dialogue, let alone forgiveness, can never develop.

Fr. Lapsley's work in Cape Town is invaluable far beyond its environs, because it shows us what the path to reconciliation can look like, not just in the face of personal trauma, but also between whole peoples with a centuries-old history of hatred and warfare.

In a nutshell, this work includes listening to people scarred by violence, whether perpetrators or victims, and helping them to deal with their emotions. It means turning them toward reconciliation, and teaching them about forgiveness. It seeks to respect the diversity of ethnic and religious cultures on our planet, and acknowledges that all people are spiritual beings and have intrinsic worth. Finally, it sees that there is no route forward without the willingness of all former enemies to share responsibility for the past, and to recognize that every human is capable of being both a victim and a victimiser.

To face oneself in such a way – to see in oneself the possibility of becoming like one's own worst enemy – is a very

Father Michael Lapsley with Bishop Onweng of Northern Uganda

hard exercise. But it is also liberating. Because as every chapter of this book amply illustrates, there is no victory without struggle, no redemption without remorse, and no healing without pain. There is no such thing as spring without winter. Unless, as the Gospel puts it, the seed dies and is buried, there will be no new grain.

In a world driven by fast-paced excitement and high-level anxiety, the long, hard work of rebuilding a village torn apart by genocide rarely makes the evening news. Similarly, as I know from my own work speaking about forgiveness in schools, an assembly on nonviolence will never attract reporters, whereas a shooting will bring a school instant and lasting notoriety. But why should success be measured by coverage or publicity?

Dorothy Day, an old acquaintance of mine who worked for decades among New York City's poor, said that in trying to change the world the biggest obstacle is never other people or institutions, but our own sense of discouragement and futility. "We *can* change the world, to a certain extent," she admonished in a newspaper column. "We can throw our pebble in the pond and be confident that its ever-widening ripples will reach around the world."

I am sure that there are more stories of love and forgiveness in the world than there are stories of hatred and revenge. How long will you wait to let yours be heard? When are you going to throw your pebble in the pond and start making ripples?

EPILOGUE

At the beginning of this book I wrote about a man who had murdered a seven-year-old girl and asked, "Can such a man be forgiven?" In the years since I first met him, he has undergone a remarkable change. Whereas at first he was emotionally numb and tended to see his crime as the inevitable result of society's ills, he later began to accept responsibility for his own actions. He began to agonise over his need for forgiveness – to weep for others, rather than for himself. Then, gradually but unmistakably, I watched as his remorse worked wonders: he was able to confront the gravity of his deeds, accept the full weight of guilt, *and* experience a remarkable peace of heart – the peace the Gospels speak of, which "transcends human understanding."

Can such a man be forgiven? If we truly believe in the transforming power of forgiveness, we must believe that he can. For even if his victim's family insists on withholding their forgiveness, redemption can also come from God – and in the case of this man, it is hard to deny the fact that he has experienced its blessing.

Of course, we can never belittle the agony his victim underwent, and the pain her family must still bear. All the remorse in the world cannot undo the crime of murder. But neither can we write off a person like this as hopeless and deny him the opportunity to change. No matter how repeatedly we ourselves stumble or fall, we still want others to forgive us, and to believe that we can change. As Jesus of Nazareth put it so many centuries ago, "Let him who is without sin cast the first stone."

Forgiveness is power. It frees us from every constraint of the past, and helps us overcome every obstacle. It can heal both the forgiver and the forgiven. In fact, it would change the world if we allowed it to.

Each of us holds the keys to forgiveness in our hands. It remains to us whether or not we choose to use them.

THE AUTHOR

Johann Christoph Arnold's books on children, marriage, death, peacemaking, and forgiving have sold over 400,000 copies in English and been translated into numerous languages. A writer with an uncommon wealth of experiences and personal insights, he is also a pastor, and has counselled (with his wife, Verena) thousands of individuals over the last thirty years, including married couples, children, and teens; addicts, prison inmates, and law enforcement officers; educators and students; and the terminally ill.

Arnold is a frequent guest on talk shows and a popular speaker at schools and conferences internationally on the role of forgiveness in nonviolent conflict resolution, and on its importance as a step to reconciliation. An outspoken social critic, he has participated in initiatives for peace and justice around the world. Recent journeys have taken him to Europe, the Middle East, Central America, Southeast Asia, and Africa – and into schools, hospitals, prisons, and refugee camps.

Arnold and his wife have eight children and almost fifty grandchildren, and live in upstate New York.

INDEX OF NAMES

INDEX OF NAMES